Terra
Nova

CRAB ORCHARD SERIES IN POETRY
Editor's Selection

Terra
Nova

POEMS BY Cynthia Huntington

Crab Orchard Review &
Southern Illinois University Press
Carbondale

Southern Illinois University Press
www.siupress.com

20 19 18 17   4 3 2 1

The Crab Orchard Series in Poetry is a joint publishing venture of
    Southern Illinois University Press and *Crab Orchard Review*. This
    series has been made possible by the generous support of the Office
    of the President of Southern Illinois University and the Office of
    the Vice Chancellor for Academic Affairs and Provost at Southern
    Illinois University Carbondale.

Editor of the Crab Orchard Series in Poetry: Jon Tribble

Cover illustration: *Terra Nova*, original oil painting, by Frank Gardner
    (frankgardner.com)

Library of Congress Cataloging-in-Publication Data
Names: Huntington, Cynthia, 1951– author.
Title: Terra Nova / poems by Cynthia Huntington.
Description: Carbondale : Crab Orchard Review & Southern Illinois
    University Press, [2017] | Series: Crab Orchard Series in Poetry
Identifiers: LCCN 2016033741 | ISBN 9780809335756 (paperback) | ISBN
    9780809335763 (e-book)
Subjects: | BISAC: POETRY / General.
Classification: LCC PS3558.U517 A6 2017 | DDC 811/.54—dc23
LC record available at https://lccn.loc.gov/2016033741

Printed on recycled paper. ♻

This paper meets the requirements of ANSI/NISO Z39.48-1992
    (Permanence of Paper) ∞

The ship? Great God, where is the ship?
—Herman Melville, *Moby-Dick*

CONTENTS

Terra
Nova

Come Now, Angel

I.

A candle in the church of the fishermen
carries the prayer of its burning
up into shadows. Smoke laces the rafters,
scrolls in air. The icons of the apostles are burning,
their carved wooden faces,
their painted wooden robes,
these fishers of men are burning, the church
is burning, flames orange against night sky.
Stained glass exploding shatters
on stone floors, that winter night.

                That winter night
when I lay on the fourth floor of the hospital,
the blinds drawn back showing rows of hemlocks
ice-shrouded above the lights along the road,
that night, the coldest of the year,
my room was warm behind dark glass.
I had a view of pine woods,
and the access road winding downhill past Emergency.
On a ward locked down for all our safety,
the violent sadness scoured my brain
until I was a fire to myself, indicted for crimes
no one had yet discovered.

I turned on my narrow bed, I could not turn
from myself to escape my fate, brought down,
brought here, by history, my story to account.
I watched the hours turn.

The night nurse, a heavy man with soft eyes,
passed down the corridor every thirty minutes,
checking into every room,
making rounds of the not-damned—they said
we were not damned. A brand plucked from the burning,
2 A.M. and the church was burning;
from four hundred miles away I watched it burn.

"I will destroy the idols and put an end to the images . . ."
Asleep on his left side three hundred ninety days,
Ezekiel counts the years of Israel's iniquity.
On his right side, forty days for Judah.
                    I did as I was bidden,
my charge to destroy the false forms, smash up
the images and violently dispel the fault—
this world of lies I was beholden to undo,
a holocaust of false relations and deceit.
To bring a cleansing chaos to the land.
My brain the fire, the world undone.

Under the warehouse on the harbor
where the building juts out over the beach,
men sleep wrapped in cardboard and old blankets
against the cold. One turns, gin-heavy,
the cigarette forgotten in his fingers,
he falls, it falls . . . longer, slow falls a spark, a smolder,
hot dark the ash burns down until it flames
to wash like wave up into boards, to lick and leap,
tongue air, to run up into beams and timbers,
burning a block of waterfront that night.
Morning, under charred timbers, glass and wire,
what's found are teeth and bones.

Coal tumbles down the chute into the cellar
of the house on the corner,
where the street turns to follow the harbor's bend.
The truck breathes smoke exhaust . . .
Black oily fossil of swamps and ferns,
Three hundred million years awaiting light.
We dig, we scratch with rake and pick,
and layers reveal more layers,

                              awaiting light.

I walk down the hallway at two in the morning.
The night nurse at her desk
in front of the barred doors, looks up, inquires,
offers sedative. I say to her: the burning,
the sweet air up from the gap in the rock,
revelation I am here to tell.

                              2.

                    Babylon. The just flee, retreat to the desert.
We flee not to escape temptation but slavery. Among rocks and wild
honey the spirit rests, and Babylon is bright, it is cruel, and brightly
beautiful, offering all we cannot hold—not for us this shine and dazzle.
Money and power are theirs, song and sweet fruits dripping juices on the
chin. We turn to the rocks and the wild sky, the well in the desert, its
water cold and pure
                    —but the little cafés with flowers hanging in pots
from hooks, blossoms cascading—and the guitars playing, and a woman
with upswept hair—the back of her neck white and tender there—it
seduces, it would intoxicate, there we would forget our God—but if you
have no money or power it is not for you,
                    your hands smell of shellfish and oil, gasoline
and sweat—what is Babylon to the conquered? We were slaves in
Babylon, who once were sovereign nations and proud. The guitar and
tambourine, the perfume and sweetmeats are not for us—

O it intoxicates, it swells and gleams! But not for us, godly and poor—rather go to the desert, or walk beside this restless ocean—back to the beginning of what was ours. Sold, conquered, we may not take it back. It breaks us, it breaks us down, the harbor, the woods where we played as children, the graveyard, the church burned to its foundations, all our secrets violated, every sacred place taken over, the memory sears . . .

3.

for dorothy bradford

And for the season it was winter. . . . What could they see but a hideous and desolate wilderness, full of wild beasts and wild men. . . . If they looked behind them, there was the mighty ocean which they had passed and was now as a main bar and gulf to separate them from all the civil parts of the world.

William Bradford, *Of Plymouth Plantation, 1620–1647*

Now you want to turn from the cold, from the wind peeling up off the harbor, slapping the benches and making the street signs chatter. The water's surface hard, a poverty of light: the ocean is stone, is iron, is a winter field frozen six feet down. Graveyard of boats and bones. High tide swirls over the great stones of the breakwater, rubble mount of the dike. Last winter a girl was swept from the rocks and drowned. Men tried to save her. All day the drum beats on the rocks, calling her bones out from the cold waters: hear it banging the skin of the sand, thrum and slap.

Walking beside the breakwater, past the salt marsh, bleached grasses shake and flinch and start up as if electrified. Now the wind finds you, reddening your eyes, blows the tears back and scours your face. The ache in your jaw will not unclench. Now you want to turn, but the wind follows you, it seeks you out. You in particular, queried and pressed by cold. Weather's inquisition: *where are you broken, where can you break?* A gap becomes a breach that floods the channels, overwhelms defenses; it will find you out. The germ will prosper to a colony, make outpost in the lung; the cut will not heal, the flesh blisters and fever stalks the blood. This cough that settled in my chest and means to stay.

And out on the rocks a child crying, fretful, clutching her father's knee; she swats at the arms that would lift her and whines, a long note the gulls carry up, that cry the sky can't hold sounded over and over.

Five weeks the ship lay at anchor, and then the dying began, the sickness taking one after one. None who did not cough that first winter, weaken and fall. Some rose again, others not. First Edward Thompson, young manservant to William White. Then the boy, Jasper More, fell into his bunk with fever and died after eight days. This infection, the "ordinary sickness" as they called it, would kill nearly half the colony, saints and strangers alike before spring.

The More children: Eleanor 8, Jasper 7, Richard 5, and Mary 4 were sent here to be gotten rid of, indentured to strangers after their mother's fault unfathered them. "A spurious brood," he branded them when he charged their mother with adultery. Not content to disinherit, he must disappear these children he would not own. Three of them would die that winter, only Richard surviving.

It was Dorothy who nursed the motherless boy in his last sickness; two days after his death she slipped over the side of the *Mayflower*, or let herself down, and drowned. They buried the child on shore, but no one saw the woman fall—one step into the night, she swirled downward and did not cry out, or if she cried her cries were not heard in that December night, here, just past where I stand.

Dorothy's husband, William Bradford, off exploring the Cape would return to find his "dearest consort" gone. Her body never recovered, her name expunged from all his journals.

Her desolation in the days before, nursing the dying boy, her own son John, only 3, left behind in Leiden. What saints, what freaks, what insult to nature in their fanatic creed. There was madness among them, winter hanging in a darkening sky, and the epidemic gaining.

Now you want to turn, and turning, find the self, the you, before this bar, this gulf, was opened. When does pilgrimage become exile, the peregrine self feel self as refugee?

Oil of night, the ocean takes you whole and you are no more. Then you are wholly ocean. Currents sweep over, leave no trace, mixing and stirring, pressing onward. If your father will not own you, you are no one. These are our forebears: a cast-off child and a heartsick woman. A man walking toward the interior of a strange country, carrying an oar over his shoulder like a musket, stealing Indian corn. Theirs not the first exile, first betrayal or act of war, this history writ here early, inscribed on this shore. Still ours somehow, with all that would come after.

4.

Were you dreaming then? Walking the old streets, but no one knows you there? Thinking you could return, but all the dimensions have shifted. People stare as if they would insult you, a three-legged dog hops across the gutter wearing your grandmother's false teeth hung from his collar. The bell tower they have painted orange, chain-link festoons the entrance to the park. A smell of cigar smoke: it was that dream where you want, with all that you can muster of your tired heart, to get back to something that's gone for good. Then turning home, to where you still think of home, and the street ends at an abandoned baseball field grown up with weeds. You're crying *stop, I was here before, this is mine!* The wraith of a fisherman looks through you, you knew him once in Carthage, now he's sunk in dementia, carrying a folding chair and humming fado.

Met here, our archangel Christobal, fallen to earth, reeling. Christ bearer, holding the weight of the world inside him, doomed and damned to walk the long street raving—the bottle in his coat pocket—he drank as if he were sentenced to drink, the scripture of his sorrows he read aloud in the dark.

You get one native land, once, and that's it. I know I've lived my life on stolen ground, on sacred hills of a vanished nation, walked over graves and broken faith. The heartbreak of ghosts, who say the living stink. I was innocent, doomed to trespass; like you I have no home—no place someone hasn't bought with their blood, and still the generations migrate as birds—or not as birds, since birds do not carry sorrow.

5.

song of iron

I will eat this loneliness. It is heavy food
cooked in an iron skillet over coals. Dust clinging to rafters, cobweb
under a stairwell, black dust of miners who died gasping for sky. Rock
of the heavy ages. Why am I born here free, a wanderer without home?
In every generation we are called to leave, led through the wilderness
extravagant, led off the strata, vagrant, unable to see past the single day
over and over, carrying our invisible God.

Eat loss. The house gone, the marriage
broken, the lover fled. Gap in the earth waiting to receive you. What is
learned from this journey: that two worlds are one? Is it enough? Wild
roses in a paper cup, white moons of a woman's fingernails, a hand
writing with a silver pen *I am.*

6.

comrade

And we could talk all night propped on pillows, the one blanket
pulled over our knees . . . gin with ice in cups, no lamp, we lay back we

reclined replete still vibrating with touch warm and cool, our voices low
and steady, gazing until our eyes in the dark could see souls.

Morning, salt air drafted up from the harbor, and entering our rooms,
a freshening, like another world coming into you. *Whoomp* of a car door

falling shut, and steps on gravel crunching like stones at the far waves'
edge, clattering one on another, stone smoothing stone.

Is there forgiveness in dream, I need to ask you? Does the harm I've done
outlive me, or is there, finally, an end to all this grief birthing grief?

Some place where it plays itself out and subsides, like storm waves folded
back into the harbor, the simmer and pop as sand percolates, and takes

each blow in separate streams, back into underworld of ocean, the forces
of that violence dispersed. And I remember, I am reminded, by grace,

how no single particle is a violation of trust, how, broken up, the endless
matter of the world is gentled, things returned to their elements,

how uncreated we are without sin. Light then, and the small leaves of the
aspen breathe their tremble joy and dance in air, which is the felt

presence of God in the world, *within* the world, in our being entire as
matter burned with light, which is a pillar of cloud and a pillar of fire,

which is the beloved who rests in the smallest space between the leaf and
its shadow on the wall. We are, as we were, these lovers, this beloved.

Scattered my words in air, as light dividing colors in a bead of rainwater.
How light falls on the ground and lies there pooled, shimmering up,

but the dark beneath the disk of leaf shadow falls inward forever.

7.

harbor

From the beginning this shelter,
the harbor cupping a depth
that was passage and return,
that was food and men's labor.
The tough boats that made a fleet:
strength it gave to the town, a being.

For hundreds of years the boats going out.
The town to serve them then,
to fit out, crew, supply, unload,

pack fish in the cold storage, gut and slice,
scales glittering in piles you wade through
in high boots, slick underfoot.

They were hard years, hard generations.
Run out to the bend when sails were spotted:
half-masted meant a man was lost.

What was lived here can't be bought,
but what was owned is taken,
what was built falls to strangers. It floods me,
filling, overfilling, this grief
a deepening darkening, overcome.

Still, blueberry, beach plum, cranberry,
bay and sassafras, boletes in fall.
And behind the close-shouldered houses
kitchen gardens with shell borders,
salt hay mulching kale and potatoes,
tomatoes reddening, a lilac tree
waving branches, this richness folded
into interstices, the firmness of objects.

I walk and the streets, the houses,
furl within me, mapped in cells, awakened,
contained and opening. The town
with its stories and structures, its history
and legends, is in me, as we are in our dreams
even as they are inside us.

It comes back to the harbor
which is always to be beyond,
to be ventured and to receive.
A depth, and a surface of light,
contained and limitless,
against which portal we are shades.

II

The Back Shore

I.

back shore dawn

long sigh of waves breaking
        along the whole shore pulse from far out a single beat
    in one rush turned back scattered confusion flusters

     of foam
   the push then another behind
                      bears up on berm—gulls cry
       overhead slow lament and drift from sand hills down
to flats where tide falls down away the seabed covered
                   uncovered reveal
re-veil repeats
        through eons unwitnessed
            sand seethes
   and footprints swell dissolve pulled under
                ocean under

   beach world floats on water
        current folds into
    itself raises up pulls under drowns
  this vision then another
        ghosts of sailors fade

                              at dawn sink under
wave to vanish.

              Angel of night return
and carry those who stumble
                        wrestle
the damned back into their bodies
          make them hear remembering voice of voyages

                          2.

                                          night fishing

All night casting into the waves.
Quick rushing clouds, chips of moonlight
blown across shallows,
waves tossed between bars
where bass are running,
or bluefish mob a school of mackerel.
Foam and slash of water black with blood.

Dawn, the fish swim into deeper water;
the men turn away, stowing rods and coolers,
loading gear into truck beds.
Tide's collapse swallows their tracks,
opening sinkholes, caverns to underworld
where carcasses of wrecks lie bound.
Viking, slaver, pirate, every fugitive villain,
these criminal conquerors, usurpers of world,
pound like blood in the quiet, are pounded under,
are wave and sand, are ship's skeletons,
are chests of gold and pearl.

A truck starts up, thrum and growl,
lurches down the beach,
pitched side to side in ruts.

You hear the engine catch and start up loud,
then quiet gone away, then waves.
Water spills into water washed, waves
swell and break; these sounds are with you
as you surface, breach in air.

Light will not surprise your dreaming,
that knows, better than time,
how worlds dissolve. Wake now to this one,
slow shunt of vapored air, salt weight of wet;
how being rests upon you mild,
and twines its arms at your neck,
and leans its weight upon your breast.
Spirit speaks as sigh, whispers: *I go.*
The window dilates, giving beyond;
a blue-gray shadow on a blue-gray wall:

> *Oh stay!*

lover now hand hair-twined fingers hold,
> and blackbird sings

his sharp waking cry;
> day breaks in rattling and new,

bearing up limbs of time in its arms.

3.

in tongues

Then morning, a room of windows. My house a single cell, dividing
immensities. Ship of space within which being hums. I'm toasting bread
over a gas burner, turning it over and back, pinched between tongs. Blue
flame licks goldening bread. Don't tell me the story of wheat. I was there,
gleaner after the harvest. *Euphrates.* Or the gift of fire stolen from sun,
stored in bodies that lay buried for eons. Cell, flesh, bone, we breathe the
dead, we warm ourselves at the fire of them, we handle their tools, stone
and iron, and repeat the story of wheat, which made cities. Long rains
wakening the plains, undoing the earth, her constant sorrow. Thunder

batters the hills. A stick, a rake, a plow. *Einkorn. Emmer.* And I am, the
soul is, the germ in the seed, held secret, warmed by sun in darkness, the
gift of time, the gift of fire, repeating in it, through it. In earth darkness
the seed will crack and split, the cold underearth water pressed forward
seeking opening, *not yet, not yet* . . . now *fittzz* up my veins, hot-wire
sparklers bright against black, lightning forks along the nerve, a charge
leaps the gap and I fall. Brain fires flash and stutter. Into the gap, the
chasm, ground split wide, spirits whisper their hum of promise, every
impulse carrying messages. Voices enter and I fall. I fall, and what green
shoot springs from my side?

4.

What branch, what leaf?
In fit I fell, a gap cleft mind
and other issued forth. I am not I.

How power quivered then in everything,
and if I put my hand out I could feel the charge
            inhabiting every object—chair back, a wineglass—
like a live wire and you could dance
with this power/ force/ energy
steer/ sail/ take the burn
and rearrange the world

and there were secrets to be found out
and secrets to be sliced open and revealed
in daylight, forces without wires or cords
flung into time, received over
and over, forever constellated
to be called up, genie
obedient but blank and literal waiting
                              word.

God's not in the human.
A voice says: *daemon is not of mind.*
Groping here to say

the image afflicts, it is
invasion, no melody, the vision torments,
it is the vast below
come through the break, all creation howling.
. . . *voice without utterance . . . without the sound of words*

5.

Green lash of snake sped into high grass
gone out from me, no mark.

The way a fish swimming underwater leaves no wake.

Have you seen how a kingdom is made and unmade?
Have you heard the oracle's cries of prophecy?
The kings of ancient time were dead and this world built
on ten worlds that were broken before.
We all shall be raised, we shall be changed,
we shall hear angels.

But first the exile, first the captivity,
then the turning back.

6.

the deep

God's not in the human,
yet mind arises out of matter.
The land rose up
                    piecemeal, speck and particle,
rock and grain,

          as it is still appearing, given from waves
                with offering of sand,
                        each earth crumb and pebble churning.

The separation of the land from the *Un-*.
Sea's floor an original landscape,
hills and plains, complete. Until land is ventured
in air, the first exile.

Then thousands of years no one came. The waters
lay empty, unbroken. How could world know itself?

Its sound which is motion, its beat which is time,
matter against matter humming, hymning,
                                        that measure
enters every cell. All beings
alive and not alive, created and noncreated,
stone, air, mollusk, fish and cloud, receive repeat
one message of pulse to particle.

Within each wave the wellspring of wave
sent forward and refused
thrust and turned aside
the arriving meeting the resisting,
that would be fixed, but nothing is fixed,

world out of balance, forever shifting, flowing
at various speeds, urge testing form.
And we may be destroyed, be scattered and blown,
ocean in everything unreal body,
created and uncreated, with or without.

The gulls cry over the water,
and stones smash back and forth.
Water washes their dust and they shine, diminishing.

7.

argonauts

Sailors and fishermen, sailors and fishermen,
our forebears and fathers
in flickering light of whale lamps, torches,
the nets hauled up the winches groaning,
the wheel the compass the sails weighing wind.

Older than the makers, before iron or cloth,
the boats going out. What they gave/ carried/ made—
rough coasts and strange cargoes, sailors pressed into service.
Servant women with bundles, bearing blood.
The rescue, the surfboat launched into the storm,
the wheelman sighting land after weeks at sea.

Pirates, fanatics, whalers, rumrunners, captives,
the moving and mingling of tribes, of trade and carnage.
Attack on the enemy asleep in their tents; a city razed.
Ark, coracle, schooner. Star map, sextant and compass;
celestial navigation, the merchandise of empire,
discovery of worlds. And the net dragged up the side,
heavy with fish, our ancient food.

*   *   *

Across the gap, the impulse flares,
charging the world of matter.
They bring messages, always messages—
in the mouth, in the ear, in the body,
in microbes of plague and seeds of beach rose.
Form forever in flux, messenger angels.
Words, and the breath that carries words.

No still place through which the moving moves,
the space between the leaving and the arriving,
where spirits enter. Always a gap.
Time unmarked by leaving, by comings and goings,
though the quick hours devour themselves.

Ezekiel thunders in the waves.
We have his book, chewed up and spit out.
He says God says we are rebuked.
The boats float heavy into harbor,
carrying prisoners—captives, slaves—
strange cargo. And we shall build
                              Jerusalem
on this inheritance.

Brass buttons,
and a woman's parasol, fluted with sand.

*   *   *

A woman sits in a chair by a window in sun,
an infant on her lap, and she is singing
a song about voyages, sailing in a teacup,
a pinecone tossed on the current, rocking him
who can't hold his head up, or find his mouth
with his fingers, whose eyes
fix her face for all world.

The Book of Paradise

Before there was time, there was water, and a darkness covered the deep.
Bruce Feiler, *Abraham*

I.

Before there was light there was wind, and it rained on the newborn earth four million years. The cloud vapor was so thick no sunlight reached the earth. We were burning, even the rain could not cool us. On ourselves we rained, in one self we burned—our self was all one mass and all we are was present then, already understood. There could be no thought yet of continents or seas, no forest, fern, or bog, nothing living and nothing to live upon. But everything was. Molten rock, that great creation soup, simmered, bubbled—take and eat. It was my body. There is a planet that is a diamond. It lies near to us in our own galaxy, this Milky Way, Path of Ghosts, the stepping-stones that spirits follow through the spiral out onto the other edge, the nothing before being. This diamond planet laid along their way rings like a gong in space, it chimes an aching high note; they must not stop there but continue on, the lonely, last, difficult, desired leaving that is return, and it is said they begin to remember as they approach, to long for what they came out from, stars and darkness. Then they are glad. Not they, but us. We are those spirits finding our way without eyes. Before there was light there was wind and it was a new earth. And before this earth, there was no wind, we could not rain on ourselves, we had not begun, and, unfallen, we knew no path to rise.

Born the worms in crawling swarms. Born the mites,
the small worms which turn the earth. . . . Born the eggs
in the sea without number, born their striped children.
"Po wale ho-i (Still Night Everywhere Reigning),"
Hawaiian creation song

Born the worms in crawly swarms.
Born in mung the sea worms pink
swimmers wriggled wet entwined
in knot of rot the weedy paste
grease-reeking nest roiled up onshore.

Gulls wade the edge feet black,
black muck they tug at tangle to unwind
long swallow flailing down gull throat.
Bark choke and gag—ack ack the cries.

Born vegetable seed and germ.
Born ocean. Born of night the swarm
creation shadow earth dreamed down
uprisen simmer swelling gasses stew.

Stinks in sun, this creation.

first birth

I was the world. Then I was in the world.
The blood cord cut I cried
                    to breathe.
Through lungs and mouth world comes in rush.
Must not be probed or cut;

do not cross section, stain or
      sample, but breathe deep, and smell
the marshy scent of infant's head,
      still soft bone nest
with vessels' pulse and blue
translucent skin stretched fine.
The world I was
before I was within
         the world, lay curled inside my cells.
Each being born performs the coming forth,
enfolds the all unfold.
I was the world, and mirror of the world.
Remember this.

Then light—did I neglect
to mention light?—awakened ghost.
I twitched like frog, my cocked knees kicked,
my spine bucked stiff to arch. A new
sensation being self, a one to organize, conduct
an inside and an out. Those days were hard,
a test. I howled. I was the world, and chaos
reigned, a storm, the universe in every cell,
that overwhelm.

4.

the garden

The shekinah was in the garden
because the shekinah was the garden.
In leaf and root incarnate, she
was fruit and flower, she
was secret cause and groundswell to engender
life in death. The seed must fall.
How else could new-made world be greened,
the earth be nest?

Some softness, yet the will of seed and husk
to press and break, provide
a place to ripen, rest, and swell.

Life's in the flower.
Tree of knowledge spun from light,
we breathe by green. By grass, leaf, vine,
from dark, from underwater, dirt of time.
All past and future in the seed,
how time transparent opens green,
the flower undone.

The Elohim carved out
the day from night, the firmament
from earth and did not speak again.
They left a wild, a lonely place.
She wove the parts with filament,
leaf canopy, moss-bedded streams,
the secret rock under God's sun, the bed.
The secret under God's one sun is sex,
is seed and flower—blossom *is*
seduction, one must tend
the garden or find wasteland there.

And wisdom was in the trees
that live beneath the earth as deep as sky
their record of beginnings, script and scroll.

He was the word. She was the song,
shaped in the throat, tasted on tongue
and lips, oh pray, a space
for us in time, a garden earth
where world first breathed.
Who broke them? Did we live before?

5.

God is mild today, he is like a brother or a friend.
You can approach very near but you will find he has no edges, you will be
always approaching, never quite able to touch—always that is the way;
he retreats before you, drawing you forward, alluring, receding, effaced,
until you find you have entered him and been caught up. That is always
the way with him.

How he breathes in and out, how he takes the
blue of the great arching sky into his silk-shiny surface. He manifests, he
hides and reveals. He is the disappearing sky, the sky that always begins
just past your reach, and the soft, still unyielding sand, but he is most
alive today, most felt, best known, splashing almost waveless here where
I walk, leaving little ridges of sea foam and shells at the water's edge.

You think you might touch him but you will not.
If you put your hand in the water the body of water disappears. There is
water but where is the ocean? The water surrounds your hand without
itself changing, it swallows you up and is calm, you leave no mark in it
and when you take your hand away the cold feels like a fire searing your
skin but the water gives no sign.

God is bright on the surface, endlessly deep.
We cannot breathe in him. He breathes the world. See how the prints
of the little birds go down to the beach, go toward the edge of the water
and disappear.

You are in him already. Enjoy me, he told Saint
Teresa, loosen the bonds of your flesh. Ungird your loins for chrissake.
This fine blue day, he says, enjoy me. He whispers he will give me
everything. Here is a stone, rubbed smooth, a bit of shell, some fish
bones. Bits of your broken world, he whispers, approaching so gently as
foam at water's edge, dissolving, falling back. Hiss. Hush. No pursuit.
He says: you are mine. In him already. I am wet with him, blue with his

sky, breathing the breath of his breath—he does not drown or grasp or try to pull me in, to make me gasp for air, spitting sea foam and cold rant of prophecy. He stays near me on the shore, he gives me a place to stand. A little while.

6.

snake dance

in descant shiver shrink
        the lovely densities
        of flesh my bones made small

self held to self drew in   the sheddy skin
                                hug breath slid out

my skin   made fresh   again pale cream
unwritten page   new rinse of flush

translucent tender   slight/ light's
                        membrane
        water's wash

touch marks me once   in time to ripen/ fall
and rise spring gold   then seem
to quit   grow mere
wrinkle in was
                the gap   from out confined
        go into vast

into that leaving all
        made small unfurl

7.

what the serpent knew

1. That God had lied regarding the fruit of the tree.
2. That a question divides knowing and unknowing.
3. That knowledge of self breaks an order, and is suffering.
4. Further, that suffering is consciousness.
5. That a part of self not known as self struggles to be seen.
6. That world unchanging dies.
7. That the woman, who was made through first division, a part, the lesser portion of the Adam, must desire reunion.
8. That she carries the seed of life in her desiring and must be furthered.

Autumn. The lowering dark. Open your eyes. Few leaves shimmy in this Canada wind. (*Kanata: a settlement. Shimmy: in old French, chemise or shift, a woman's undergarment.*) We are in the world again. UN-made.

Let the silk strap fall
         from your shoulder soft
to allure. There must be
     resistance to seduce,
            to lead astray, away.
Oh come aside
and I will tell you all my secrets
here.
        (Oh *pissh*, you shall not surely die!)

IV

The Tenth Island

down with the boats

Wind tearing my hair, whipping tears
from the corners of my eyes: the pier
moving underfoot. Sway and rise
and fall from under, the live,
gray-green water slapping the pilings,
sloshed up the sides of the boats, remnants
of the great fleet: *Terra Nova*, *Little Infant*, *Pat
and Chico*, *Second Effort*, small tough boats
fitted out for open sea. What we built.
It's about to rain. Cars nose
and nudge onto the narrow street,
the parking lot emptying of day-trippers.
The highway takes them, peristaltic, slow,
and in a while the town
is a small town again. The boats rise,
lifted on tide; *pong* of mud and fish
and diesel, smells like the past. We were so poor
the voices say over and over
and we came here and we were poor again,
but always the tough men
wrangling the nets the ropes those whalers
and fishers and builders of boats, we came

25

with clothes on our backs, thought we would return
with trunks full of money until years
the town became us, we buried our dead
in the ocean, bones and buttons, we buried
our dead on the hill above town, but the town is gone,
sold away, the fish are gone, fished out,
the island was lost, the harbor claimed, a city
built a city lost, I'm down here with the boats,
rain sputtering up in gusts, wind lifts
the water off the harbor sprayed up and the blue
sheen of oil floats, spread across the surface,
thin like gold leaf, will not mix.

2.

from: the lost fathers

      We are wanting a father because we are poor. Our father said nothing against our sacrifice. He sent us into the woods, left us in the night with no fire. Our father said nothing. He went on a boat. He sat with the old men, drinking whiskey. We were wagered and lost to the gypsy. He turned his head away. He closed the shop and went into a back room to work on the intricate gears of machines. He called Sunday evenings. He went into the north where there were mills. We never heard word. Daddy. We sat at the table and there was no food. The house was dark, the bank calling on the telephone. A bucket of fish from the wharf. Papa. *Pai.* He married and made new children. We are poor and hated. We try on bridal dresses in a shop and stare into the long mirror. Veiled, we are lovely, disappearing. Lacy sleeves like wings. The angel stands at the door, bearing a letter. Our father died clutching his heart in an alley. We think at the last minute he called our name.

3.

The women pray and cover their heads,
eat bread and salt.

And one walks down to the wharves at night
to drink whiskey with men and laugh
leaning back. Low tide, sweet stench
of the other world, taste of sin:
strange spice, the musk of want.

She climbs into a car with the god of death
who offers smoke in the mirror,
sighs her mystery, whispers her lovely,
eyes darkened with mascara, with bruise,
croons her ember and ash.

His hair slicked back, black streak of gloss,
his teeth white and even and small.
Turn up the radio, music from hell.
Sweet ache like a wire in your heart,
twisted when he smiles, he touches
your breast, you swoon
into him, go down, go down.

4.

the idiot

Leaves swaying against green shutters,
the blind half-raised; its slats uneven across the glass. Chipped paint
flakes on the sill, curled and crimped like old leaves. The glass shines,
rippling green in sunlight, the sky floating upside down between the
branches.
　　　　　The secret of the window, both hiding and
revealing, leaves sway, reflected in glass—two worlds, within and
without. The oddity of a window, how it teases vision, darkens and
reflects. Consider the uncanny nature of mirrors, which swap right
for left but not up for down, and always reflect us at half our size. The
reflection does not make nature self-aware; the mirror means nothing
without us, though we turn self-conscious before it. I gaze into the glass
and touch my face. Why don't I touch my image in the mirror, the other?

Bamboo climbs to the top of the window frames. Underneath, spiky purple flowers sprout up from stone. Such perfect quiet this morning, no one in the street, only the leaves swaying. Inside that house is the dummy—the *bruxa*'s idiot son. She got him from lying with some god. Now middle-aged, clumsy and shuffling, mute, misshapen, he stays at home, hidden, sometimes glimpsed by neighbors.

He stays inside or in the back. Digs in the yard, stabbing into the hard ground with a shovel and mounding up dirt in piles, later going back to fill in the holes. He sweeps the walk, swishing his broom back and forth over the same five concrete slabs for hours. The broom brushes sand from the slab, then picks up more sand when he drags it back.

Scowling, silent, he stays there, pent in his body, while she, mortal, disappears at will. Shape-shifter, lifting into air as owl, running down the road at midnight among coyotes, calling from tree branches on moony nights. But he, the god's son, waits in his own flesh forty years, growing slow and heavy. She clips his hair and nails and dresses him in man's clothes, ties his shoes.

He shows himself to little girls—yes, like that—soft, cradled in his hand like a small animal—see? His mouth gapes, witless. We would go to the gate and stare, and hide ourselves by the tulip tree. We fear him, he is harmless, his mother leaves him there alone; his loneliness is immense.

Where does she go? Into the wild chasm. Like lightning into a cloud. Into the woods beyond town. Past the abandoned houses, the hidden cemetery where the smallpox victims were buried, out along the back shore where waves from Greenland pound the beach. She returns hard-eyed and fierce and will not speak, or shrieks at some mess he leaves, another blunder or stumble, then feeds him like a bird from her hand, as he moans gently and follows her with his eyes.

Later he will disappear, just walking off one evening along the old fire road, to wander through the woods and into the barren swales, go off and leave no trace, called back to the hills by his father. Don't we know that the idiot belongs to heaven? And we who have seen him know the captive is redeemed, the visible disappears, and the glass is empty of that image it held so long, released, though his mother's howls assail the garden walls for years of nights thereafter.

5.

Men leave. In hard times they leave harder. Not all men, not the best men. Men who still believe a second chance can save them. Boys still, so full of need they can't know how they are needed. Women slam cupboards and bank the fire. Children gather in the afternoons and make up stories. The town a spiral through which they wander, passing themselves at every turn. A girl grows old waiting for the father she lost, who, after all, lost her. A boy grows up with a cloud in his vision, unable to see himself as the father rises in his face, appearing out of him in morning light unsparing—but surely he is not that, he cannot be that father, he is the forgotten son, the pain still raw. His mother looks at him and turns away. *You have his eyes.* She says this as if he has stolen something.

And no one ever leaves this story. The children go on telling it, they long for the old times but when they speak, their memories are so bitter words curdle on their tongues. Stories of abandonment, hurt, hunger, and cold, stories with no joy in them, but they say over and over how they want to return. At night they talk to one another and name the streets and say which house they lived in, these careful memories like maps, gone over again and again with no way back.

They think if they go back, they will find their fathers. They think their mothers will become kind then, and spread jam on a piece of bread held out. To taste something sweet from the mother, bitter for so long. To know the salt of father watching over.

6.

prophecy

Strangers will live in our houses and we will become their servants. Floors we swept clean every evening after supper at a kitchen table will be painted over. Empire will raise up monuments and mansions for the conquerors. Our boats will slide under the water of the harbor without remark. Surely there is a psalm for this lament.

We will make small fires at the edge of the city and turn our backs to the lights, hunkering down along the old railbed under the small twisted trees. The old ways will not be kept; we will be buried without the right ceremonies and without unction. Grass will grow long over our children's graves. All that we built, all we remembered, disappears . . . we welcomed them, we took them under our roofs and treated them as guests, now we are made beggars and slaves. We are their hands and feet.

The poor are blamed, and we blame ourselves. But how were we to live? Fishing, there was one thing that could be sold over and over, eaten and given, sold and traded, and always renewed. A miracle, paid in lives and sweat. The miracle was not cheap but we claimed it.

Then we had only one thing to sell—that could be sold only once—the birthright. Selling your harvest you are made rich, a harvest renewed. Selling your fields you are made beggars. We blame ourselves. But what was left for us to live?

Before the money came—before new people with money came and took our houses—oh that was nearly the last thing—it had been happening a long time, we were working and didn't see . . . the war for this place, this life, already lost. The big factory boats taking the fish. The price of oil and war. The price of a man's or a woman's labor not enough to bargain squarely. We dream we are a free people but we are inside empire; we can't see it for standing so near.

Living here so long, in our own ways, we thought we were free, but dominion surrounded us and we were owned before a single paper was signed. The fate of the poor always. And one by one, slowly, the widows sell off their houses, the children sell all their inheritance, what looks like choice already resolved. Hard work, but work can't help when there is no work. Hard labor then, in a town poor and rough. Work for the owners and there is never enough to bargain. A man's or a woman's labor is sold over and over until the man is worn out, the woman bent down, but the house can only be sold once and it is gone. We do not own our lives.

"I was staying that winter down at a place we called the Bethel, which was a hole-up where we crashed between fishing trips, a couple of rooms over a garage down on Cat Shit Alley. Some guys from New Bedford were laying over after a storm blew up and drove the boats into harbor. We partied like sailors all night, it got pretty crazy and some time late, after midnight, one of our 'guests' pulled a knife and punched it into the table right between Len's fingers. Len took some umbrage then, hauled himself up, stumbled over to the corner and pissed in the guy's duffel lying there open on the floor. Fortunately everyone was too drunk to do more than yell and shove each other around, throw a few swings then pass out on the mattresses.

"Morning, everyone sour with beer and bad vibes. The New Bedford guys were talking together in low voices while the one guy ran his bag under the shower. Tony walked into the kitchen, took one look and pulled Len over, told him: Get the hell out of here. Go be invisible. If we're lucky these ass-wipes will leave and not come back. He could see it coming down; these guys seemed bad—but so did our guys, and Len left and nothing happened. We almost wished something would happen.

*   *   *

"Morning down at the harbor, stale breath, no sleep, the air all innuendo of tides and past lives. Ghosts moving in the grainy dawn, the shapes of your friends flickering vague in the sea fog, everyone a shade with a flare of cigarette at his lips, sucking smoke. A woman walks out on a balcony; her arms crossed over her chest, she looks like a caterpillar in a big chenille robe, wild hair frizzed out gray, her gaze riding straight ahead to Long Point just appearing out of the clouds.

"Everyone always looking to sea. This was a couple months after the dragger went down off of Pollock Rip, nine men lost, we knew them all. Only six bodies had been found. Every day waiting for news. Not wanting to go out but never saying so. The first week, one boat, the *Paulie B*, was pulling up its nets and there was the captain, Phillie, hanging by his boot, looking up at them with frozen-open eyes. What a thing to find.

"Tony dead now twenty years—heroin—the rest of them God knows. Some memories are bad, some things mornings keep bringing back like it or not. And here we are. No more fishing fleet. In town this morning I hear the news three times, Old Mac, the one we called Chicken, killed in a fight with police up in Framingham. They tased him and he had a seizure and fell down dead. Just died, right there in the grass next to his house. Eyes rolled up in his head, that was it. That wouldn't have happened here—everybody knows him since a kid, they wouldn't take his shit seriously. He'd get talked down or locked up for the night at most. Those times are gone.

"It's terrible going out those weeks after a boat goes down. You can't admit the fear. You see the water in a different way, bodies in there, ghosts of people you knew, wrecks from hundreds of years. All of it. You gotta be tough. We were young enough to still be crazy. Those days I wouldn't listen to anybody. There was a lot going on in town—a lot happening, and nothing really happening if you know what I mean. The town was a town. Not some run away from home dream or new-assed social experiment. People looked after each other and a tragedy seemed to break us all the same. It seemed to have meaning even though it was terrible. Even terrible meaning.

"I can remember when it was socially acceptable to be falling down drunk on the street. In certain circles that is. Drugs hit the town hard. They came in like an invasion and it was ruin. Ruin. I mean, nobody but me put that needle in my arm. May I be fucked to death by Superman if I say otherwise. May I get clap from a nun.

"May I piss right in the holy water, which I would never do.

"But still it was a death trip and it came down hard on the town. They started finding bodies everywhere, like a bad dream of shipwreck turned inside out. The woman in the dunes with her hands cut off, and those girls in Truro, cut up and buried in the woods. I sold to that guy who did them, before it happened I mean, and I never thought one thing about it.

"So, I was not a nice guy. Some of you will say I'm not a nice guy now but you didn't know me then. Well, some of you did know me then. If I owe you money or broke your nose or—oh yeah, lobbed a bottle at your head (Hi Mike!) I'm truly sorry. Don't bother suing though—I haven't worked in six years, I'm on psychiatric disability, which means work makes me crazy."

V

Crónica

I.

stranger

I wake at 4 A.M. In the dream I was back
in the city. The bar would just be closing.
Wet black streets under dimmed lights,
the taxi stand, cabs in a cloud of vapor.
Vinnie would lock the door,
pour a tall vodka and watch me cash out.
Hell to pay if the count was short. That worry.

Wind up from the harbor before dawn,
the old building groans and shakes.
In the bathroom mirror my face,
bathed in fluorescent glare, is blank.
I tell the face, *Be still*
and wait. The face stares back
without affect. Stranger, simulacrum.

> *How long? How long? Beloved*
> *we are clay. Waiting we waste*
> *our time, we fail.*

34

You came here dreaming, your life was lost.
You saw the ocean for the first time,
and the trees arching over the road; it was winter.

Late afternoon on the flats, the light going gray,
shapes of bodies drift across wet sand,
flattened as on a scrim. A light like pewter
burns in the spaces between objects.

People are clamming along the breakwater.
A bucket, a rake . . . a woman in oilcloth stands pointing,
showing her husband and son where to dig.
Her hand stretched from the sleeve, she turns,
fixes me in her sight. Crone and her bone finger:
Wither you. I sink in her gaze. November cold,
the wet sand squelchy underfoot,
the chill of tide rising up through my boots.

Then the café on the west end, its cracked red booths,
steam ghosting the windows.
At the bar along the back wall men sit talking.
They look up when I enter, and turn away.
Someone's boat, someone's close call,
nothing a stranger would care about.

(I know these men, have met their ghost fathers
walking the beach with lanterns, guardians of the coast
who watch over me at night, and sit at my head and feet
when the dream wakes me shouting,
and giants mutter in the tunnel of the wind
that swirls from all sides, and batters the glass,
like someone shaking bones in a jar.)

It was a scene there every night:
Jack was selling on the side, *just enough*
to keep the party going,
he'd tell me. There were drugs everywhere
and I wasn't innocent,
but I was sick, and when Eddy was stabbed
in front of the White Horse and police
brought him to us straight from emergency,
I got jumpy.

I had pneumonia that winter, then pleurisy.
At Saint Vincent's the tired intern
shook his head: fever 104.
"What is this, 1910?" I asked,
and collapsed coughing.

Just a kid then, so skinny
I kept falling through the cracks. When they busted
the restaurant crew for coke
Jack got rehab. Me they let go. I was seeing
fire-wheeled chariots already
on the scraped-raw surface of my brain.
Some days I'd sit for hours in a chair
as if a hand had wiped my mind, not moving.

I left with two suitcases,
a bus ticket and four hundred dollars.
Beach town in winter shut down.
Dollar breakfast specials before seven,
massa sovada with plum jam
and coffee in my room, afternoon,
high windows showing sky. The curve
of harbor like a sickle moon, houses staked
at the edge of space. Men in doorways
leaning out of the wind, with lighters flickering,
faces in each other's faces.

night boat

That first winter, how the wind would come up and scare the old
building with creaks and bangs, rocking as it struggled in its truss of
studs and nails. Dark came early; I sat with my books at the bare table,
my chair scuffing the floor whenever I shifted or got up to warm some
coffee at the stove. Outside, a tree limb sawing up and down in front of
the street lamp threw long, boreal shadows that leaped and fell back into
themselves, weirdly ballooning across the pavement. Reading of Vikings
who sailed here from Greenland, and explorers, this coast discovered
over and over, for thousands of years claimed, and claimed again.

Crunch of boots on gravel, someone going—where? Three bars
stayed open, the gas station on the corner . . . the Town Hall clock
striking the small hours. Some nights I would lace up my boots and walk
the short block down to the harbor. Lights on the wharf carved a white
glare from black of sky and water, the small waves lapping, opening
and closing their knife light: *nick, nick, nick* . . . oil slick washed off the
boats smeared a purple iridescence on the surface of the water and ducks
paddled softly in the shallows.

What if a boat slid in, sailing dark, cut its engines and landed a
stranger, a fugitive, who slipped over the side to flee down narrow streets
and disappear? What prodigal, unhomed by war and empire, what
comrade brother might ghost these streets, setting the dogs barking from
one house to another? I felt him at my side when I walked, the lights in
the small panes of the windows facing up to the streets, each separate life
bright and silent behind glass. I felt his shame and longing as we walked
there unseen, unhomed. But if anyone came he was not discovered,
nothing betrayed him. The ducks floated on the black water, fluttered
their wings, and settled back.

Then daylight, men shouting and hauling boxes across the wharf,
trucks bumping down the boards. People in the street pass quickly,
heads down, wind cutting their faces. Summer shops closed,
plywood blanking the windows, we dart between points of warmth.

The tide brings up bodies and leaves them stranded in light.
Rich, rank, the things that never knew this world,
that did not want to come to shore; rotting bits of fish-heads,
seaweeds, crab legs, offal, that together make the dark muck
down under the boats. The smell of methane, nitrous,
diesel mixing with water, a burn in the nostrils.

Freddy Pissola hunkers on the curb,
smoking a cigarette he bummed from another townie.
Beside the shuttered hot dog stand a woman waits for a ride,
her stare fixed hard up the street.
In the whole world, who knows where you are this day?
In this town what door, what face?
If you filled your notebooks with lines, might they be found;
might you, someday, be found inside them, stupid hope—

6.

bruxa

I follow her up the narrow stairs, bumping my toes on the shallow
treads. This house made from ship's timbers, waves' memory in their
grain. The floor's slant pitches me left and right, not an even board or
right angle in the place. I list down the hallway, brush the walls with my
shoulders.

The sharp light of winter knifes the room, tin glare through bare
trees. The sun is a star, gives no quarter. She sits bent over a glass,
scrying; no, she is looking at a photograph of a man, she holds it in her
lap, she croons, she keens, my friend, my good friend. She was legend of
beauty once, spirit of salt air and harbor dusk they say.

She takes my wrist and turns it, then opens my palm, flicks
starflower fingers out—pfft!—feels the bones, palps the fleshy mound,
snorts:
what's
the agenda, Brenda? (One eye oozing rheum,
not pretty. I'm not Brenda)—*who's*
your daddy, Maddie?
Clown act, cheap routine. Then:
I don't like that torch you've been carrying
for that man who wants to put you
in the corner. Keep you under his hat.
You ought to know better by now.
Long sigh, I bore her: *So who are you,*
anyway, you're from away.
What kind of fun you running from?

Then quiet, stops, glares sharp into my face.
She sees the sickness in my eyes and softens,
whispers: *Child, who took your ghost?*

7.

Out the old fire road,
crossing the dunes
more slowly than elephants,
or like someone driving a flock of sheep,
weaving or straying aside to inspect
terrain: vagrant, drifter, I'm tramping
in winter light, a mild day, no shadows.

              White twist of downed trees; the old forest
buried in sand,   rubbed to bone, rises, is
                                            revealed,
discloses wind's undoing.

Scuffle of bird tracks. A well, a pump,
                              a tin cup hung on a string,
scrub pine and poverty grass.
                    This back country
never settled, forever shifting underfoot,
as plastic in contour as the spirit realm.

An empty place of dream and light.
          And I am a stranger here
the way one is a stranger always in dream,
embedded, implicated, and yet other.
Knowing there is water
in this desert, beauty in this bone; if I go
to the dry ancient places, a word
will be given
              still waiting to be known.

      Green of the pitch pine, green of the bay.
      Black of the beetle tunneling bark.   Caw.
      Owl in the trunk of the blasted oak,
      let me in.   Caw.
      Grandmother, teach me
      the secrets of earth.

      Fortune-teller, tell me
      what to ask.

VI

The Book of Men

adam's aftermath

The dream ends and you wake up on the floor.
At your high window the maple
sweeps her yellow leaves across the glass: *Ssshhame . . . ssshhame . . .*

           You broke the lamp . . . and in the long night
light has scattered everywhere . . . its remnants,
points that gleam
from husks and splinters, to be gathered up.
Bulb's filament hisses like a tongue
                  tasting air. Your eyes in your head
are zoo animals darting.
               How can you gather
what makes your hands bleed?

Glare of morning now you see the light:
Your mother had no ribbon in her hair,
doubtful she bathed under waterfalls.
Small, hairy, bent, beshit. Back there at beginnings it's grim,
you're grimed. Adam's apple, Ava's ass. Clit, slit,
twat, clot. Blood in the morning's pisspot. What bitch's
bastard hast thou begot, apes' heir, damn'd spot?

We thought that we were heaven's all;
we're just a clod, our home a stone,
a craggy planet circling space.

Searching worlds' wood, what home,
what dwelling will receive you? Fall
into history, sail to Ellis or jump ship,
swim to shore/ brave brutish wilderness
rough country/ Helltown shanties/
rumrunner/ mooncusser/ find a space
in the gaps. Eva babushka/ bundles
held/ wrapped pestilent fruit/
invasive blight/ inspect at border
Abram/ emigrant/ drifter/ vagrant
chosen new father/ and the skin on my hand
so pale and thin with age, made mortal now.

Am I hideous, Jane?
Very, sir: you always were, you know.

2.

a history of god

Once God was outside us: terrible, but limited in range. He ruled a city.
We built statues and temples for him to live in. We served him as slaves
carrying water, as bees bringing pollen to the hive. He liked the odor of
human sacrifice, drank troughs of blood. You could run from him, you
could get away from his sight, but then you would be exiled, outside the
city gates, and how would you live?

Then he was invisible, and everywhere. This was first realized by nomads.
This realizing took thousands of years, a frail understanding at first. Idols
were struck down, then raised again. It was hard to feel sure of him.
He had no name, no form. A cloud by day. By night a pillar of fire. Still
outside us, he tried to draw us close with promises, though his advances
were often clumsy, and punctuated by furious rages. He seemed to collect

injustices and to offer bargains he would then renege. He didn't get along with other gods.

Gradually he allowed that the fragrance of roast lamb might please his nostrils as well as human flesh. He consented to offer law, which suggested accountability. He remained enamored of thunder and fire.

After a long time he began to whisper that he was inside us all along. Now invisible, omnipresent, and indwelling. Calling us to know him as ourselves. He answered equally to all the names of God. We were confused trying to imagine this. He was in us as we were of and in him, consubstantial, one flesh and being. There came a son who was flesh, spirit figured as breath, and the father remained, still terrible, but sorrowful with love. This compassion remained hard to comprehend and was not always supported by evidence.

The Son's tenderness made Him remember She. The Holy Ghost returns the feminine to godhead long forgot. Sophia, Shekinah, the Virgin ascended bodily into heaven by papal decree. Surely wisdom and mercy will follow, this wholeness restored: well I've been here all along a woman, burned at the stake, kept in the tent, sent forth into wilderness to die, you might have asked me.

Now he wants to be back in the world. Absorbed, indwelling, a god visible and invisible, particular and universal. The signs indicate we aren't ready for that. Two thousand years to ponder incarnation, and still the mind stutters.

3.

          In the days of the flood we rode together inside the boat and did not come up. We were locked in, corked and sealed within the dark belly of the boat, day upon day, every day a night, our stink on everything and our breath on one another's faces. Sweat, urine, shit and blood. It rocked and it rocked. We were thrown down and pitched sideways, hurled upward and dropped. Torrent and tempest, rain lashing rain, water falling into water and no solid surface to anchor.

It was dark and we could not see one another's faces; this then was all the world. We the survivors—all nations would be our descendants. Now there was no time to wonder, or to choose among ourselves. Each of us would be needed; our destiny immense. Not one could be spared. I carried within me eggs, and the code of a hundred generations. You carried within you the spark, the vitalizing sperm and the code of other generations. Whatever we would make could come only from this. Every possibility, the long past and any future, was contained in our cells and whatever we did not carry, or could not bring forth, would be lost.

It had to be dark then; we would not have been able to look at one another. What trespass, to survive the entire world. Why were we saved, and how could we bear this blessing, this awesome charge to make the world over again out of our own flesh?

*   *   *

Rain sheets the windows. Shapes like gulls' wings rush down the glass, wings in flight, a watercolor blurring outlines, oil on water. Beyond the clean glass the clean air washes itself over and over. There is not a bird or an insect or a mouse to be seen. Every living thing seeks shelter. I lie on the bed under the window, with my books and my tablet.

Two small leaks have appeared in the ceiling. One sends a slow drip to the center of the floor; I've placed a bowl there to catch it. A towel in the bottom of the bowl to muffle the time-marking drip. The door is wet, rain driven against it. How the rain finds out every opening. The beat of the drip from the ceiling counting out . . .

A plume of mist hangs over the densely hunched bayberry. Every living thing hides in its nest. The drumming of rain on roof and walls, the rushing sound of rain on windows, and the leaves shimmying. It hurries; the rain hurries down so and yet it never arrives.

*   *   *

We left everything we knew behind forever, it would all be lost, the waters rising, wind swept down. We ran to shelter and inside the ark we were held, the ark was lifted, above the trees, the houses, above the drowning, reaching bodies, mouths that could not cry out inside the black water. Below us, everything floated. Arms and legs without volition wavered in the current. Drowned eyes, drowned hair, floating horrible and limp. Even birds went down, driven under by wind, driven down by water. There was nothing to rest on.

There in the dark, inside the bucking, shivering ark, wooden, frail, fraught . . . we could not speak of what was lost. House, village, road . . . further we could not think. It seemed then that we were not saved or in any way comforted; we saw that we had been condemned to outlive our lives. Something else had a purpose in us. We did not yet have the will to mourn—our mourning when it came would be immense, bottomless, and would last forever, and we were glad for the dark then because there was hatred in each of us for the other, and how could we meet each other's faces? So much depending on each of us, and knowing that we could never be parted.

4.

abram

as stars . . . as dust . . .
I fell, and falling fell
        away
    called out from land,
from father's house, from home.
His charge: *Go out*, meaning, no longer bound
                by history, from memory unhoused.
    Unnamed then, root cut off,
skin torn for blood, to cry in air.

It is a lonely God, a desert voice in me
that sings, a wound,
a wind from nowhere scouring what clings.
        All will be new, undoing *was*.

Stirrer of dust, tearer of wave and sky ripped clean,
how should I trust
in generations I won't live to see—
      that nation now rested, mere idea,
            unmanifest, in me?

5.

dust

Then the noontime furnace. Heat shuddering up from the sand, the sky
a plate, and out in the desert the tents of the Hebrews luffing in wind,
their heavy curtains of goat hair thumping on the ropes; they lean and
pull. Dust in your throat and eyes, dry film of triturate, sweat dries in
streaks down your face. A man or a woman's robe would blow around
their ankles, and the desert god huffs and feints, harassing every corner
and strand.

               *   *   *

Down at the edge of the foredune the beach heather is blooming; the
small yellow blossoms draw bees. The air quivers with their hover and
buzz. From the dunes' crest you might look down and think to claim
whatever lay before you.

A small height may loom in the desert.

               *   *   *

Abraham waits in the doorway, watching. Three men are approaching.
This is the beginning of our story, where myth starts toward history. But
first, turn back. The sand blows up in clouds and stings your skin; you
hide your eyes with your hand. But stepping back inside there is a silent
space, a stillness. Inside the dark tent where stars blink overhead.

There is a woman inside the tent.

Abraham sat at the entrance of his tent and saw three travelers approach. Three men and they all were God. And Abraham rushed forward to meet them and fell at their feet and bowed, brought them forward, he washed their feet, gave them water to drink, begged them to come into his tent.

In the desert a figure may suddenly appear where before there was only emptiness and bare horizon. The traveler seen in the distance a speck, becomes the center of vision, the world falling away behind him, and the tent rising up from the desert floor his only destination. For the stranger to pass by, for the host to turn away, is unthinkable. Vectors connect them, their presence inside a vast emptiness draws them. Invite the traveler who is come under your care, vagrant upon far lands, and feed him and give him water to wash, and guard his safety with your life. A courtesy neither may refuse.

Before words were written, this law of the desert.

*   *   *

God came in daylight and ate and drank. Spoke promise to Abraham, and Sarah heard. What is spoken to the man who waits at the door of his tent, aimed past him to the hidden one, the barren wife shamed by her handmaid, the one withdrawn into the daylight dark, no longer awaiting news.

The woman inside the black tent woven of goat hair, whose fibers dry in noonday sun and shrink and pull apart so daylight shines like stars through myriad tiny holes above her. And she could hear, and when she heard the crazy prophecy, she laughed.

I did not laugh, she said, and lied to God.

Yes, you did laugh.

*   *   *

This God, a strange, intangible idea, an emptiness and a power. He has barely come into existence, trying on selves, from the booming thunder God to a broker in treaties; not yet the existential consciousness who will say to Moses: I will be what I will be, or from another source: I am not yet who I am not yet. Here is the God of covenant, striking bargains like a trader. Who told Abraham so many lies until he had to make good, and now Abraham's descendants are numerous as stars in the sky. Children of Sarah, and the tribes of Hagar's womb also. The legends are clear on one thing: the children of Abraham belong to Abraham.

Because of Isaac, Ishmael will be sent away.

*   *   *

I have waited a long time in the doorway, and seen such wonders. The boats and the caravans. The broken sailors and grief-ruined women have all gone on. Rachel weeping for her children and refusing to be comforted for they are no more. The earth is unmoved. And never came the stranger with the holy promise.

I have watched in the doorway, and I have gone inside to where the dark of day shows stars. The quiet interior, inside my heart the desert, immense and silent, wracked by winds. And out of the silence a promise, I will make you fruitful, you will be written into time and partake, not left to listen behind a wall. So long have we waited until laughter breaks the waiting and moves us into life where we had hesitated.

6.

the pit was empty, there was no water in it

Tell Pharaoh what I have dreamed.
That I may be remembered.
Because the story now has broken
into twelve histories, in each of which I am no more.
Sold slave, imprisoned twice,
in both homes I am dead.

My father grieves and is not comforted.
Here I am shadow on a mud wall:
world reflects as smoke. I read the secret code of signs.

Tell Pharaoh, that my dream may dream me home.
Seven years of wealth mean famine: the surfeit
flows into the lack, a dearth
draws overflow. In dream my brothers bowed to me,
I did not know that they would bend
like wheat to atone. That I would be sold.
The dream of fortune is a dream of loss.
I did not know my dream
was of my ruin. Words are design,
but what is cut away surrenders sense.
Put the broken cylinders together
that they may be read.

I dreamed the stone wall behind the prison,
pillowed with moss and ferns, held
in its cells the original cure of granite,
exile of glacial debris,
a strength to withstand rain and sun—
I dreamed the wall was built
by original craft of hands
that learned balance through trial.
I dreamed that we would build.
In that city, in that Egypt,
we would build.

7.

Breath breathed in nostrils bring life to wake.
Break now night, light cracking sky—shekinah, shekinah, descend. And
I saw that I was naked so I hid myself in the garden, away from the sun
devouring flesh.
I am not yet who I am not yet . . .

The boats are fitted out for the voyage. Sand blows along the crest above the beach. There is a woman inside the tent, listening. My son, warm-wet in my arms, blue light of world before world still glowing, God fears your clear gaze. Before time, written into time. You shall become as one of us . . . Papa. Da. Taat.

Who told you you were naked?

I laughed, and lied to God.

VII

The Prophecy of Affliction

I.

The beach was scintillate/ hard light on the sand;
photons sparked up/ from broken mirror
of water/ shatterflash/ each sliver of
surface splits the image/ bifurcate/ trifurcate
fractal flare multiplies/ reflections./ Sun
grinds sand to crystals./ Cut my feet with fire.
                                        Sun
                    a great paw weighed
                                            down
on my chest/ a weight/ a cosmos crushed.
                                        Worlds
slammed inside my skull/ ram bang/ clash clamor
                    seismic/ waves collapse
frequencies./ Now shrill/
a thousand cicadas on benzedrine
voices too quick/ too many to
separate/ all words all languages
together/ shriek of steel alarm/ my head
swelled/ blood and vessel beat and hot
pulse pound./ I lay down,
I lay down on the sand
that smelled of wet ashes./ The sea rose
up from below.

2.

I stood in the doorway of my house, shimmering. A tremor, a quake,
rose and died back, every surge burning, every pulse a flame. I held out
my hands and saw light falling through them as particles, gold needles
piercing my skin. Then moved in my sight a flash, a copper hair snagged
on rough wood of the doorframe, single, slight filament wafted on air.
This has being, exists in the world, spark of the divine light scattered at
creation. Oh miracle! I reached to gather it in, as was charged to me of
old, but my hand had lost substance. The right side of my body, burning
along the nerve, began to disappear. Atoms blinked into nothingness:
one half of the world decomposed to pixels and grains.

Then my brain began firing, sending up godly flames, new atoms forged
to change the structure of the universe. A current shot up through the
floor into my right leg, hauling me down. Grip at my ankle: the beast
fixed me in its jaws. I fell in blast, fell wrack and shudder, fell to roll and
shake, to jerk and seize. Thrust down into my body, every nerve and cell
crying prophecy. My flesh on fire, crying in forgotten tongues, saying I
am here, remember me, but not in words not in a single syllable of sense.
My fingers clenched, my tongue a coal.

3.

I have thrown fire on the world, and look, I am watching until it blazes.

I woke in the cool dark of my room,
someone downstairs
practicing "Für Elise" on a keyboard,
faltering and starting over, each note
separate in space and time
entering my brain as discrete occasion,
one beat repeating. No melody
unless the notes connect
and join in series stream, refuse
their stark autonomy and flow as one.

I pulled the blind across the window glass,
shut off the lamps, but a buzzing within
the walls persisted. Now in the air.
Electric everywhere. I was acute in every cell,
and I knew I had been given to apprehend
the sounds of gaps and absences, of clefts
and currents joining worlds, to sense
the grid that held them, to perceive an order.

Light falling on objects has no shape—
it is the property of light to make shape seen,
to give form out of its prime neutral, its even gaze
on broken world. A gnosis perhaps.
I lay entranced on my right side, not sleeping,
keeping watch from the other side of sight.

I am not whole, I am not of this world. I hang
in the aura, the brilliance of sky inside me blinding,
in my shadowed room, awaiting.

4.

I fell through a hole in the sky to get here,
cast down. Sickness is mirage.
Now the star who stands
in the right corner of my window, this star,
which I have reason to believe has died
these thousand years, is speaking,
her voice a hum; she speaks with the android voice
of the phone company; she is speaking Sumerian,
which I have been given here to understand.
Her star voice says: *We have died, but God is.*

This gave me no comfort.
The image of God is unclear.
The image of God has a shadow;
it is not I AM. Trust nothing

of eye or ear. It is shadow. Without eye
or ear you know nothing; knowledge
comes by the body—absolute—
yet the body has a shadow, and IS NOT.

The kings of ancient time were dead
and the earth lay desolate.
This life remembered as I dreamed.
We were searching for scattered sparks.
We had to gather up the broken pieces;
we had also to be broken. Know that in time
all things end, but everything does not end in time.
The cup you hold in your hand is already shattered;
this world has died before it was made.
The star that is no more
must prophesy. How can I bear my mind?

5.

I lay on my side under the broken walls,
sky deep blue with one star: a planet, I suppose.
Darker here inside the ruins' shape—dark edged by sky,
rising. Light passing through my body
became particles, jagged slivers of gold, bright agony.

I thought my flesh was stone, but it is not stone. I thought my bones
were ash, but here they live. By order of the word—I would not call it
grace—a noise, a wind and then a rustling: *Come from the four winds oh*
breath, and breathe on these slain that they may live.

A certain monastery would begin a monk's initiate by lowering him
down a well then pulling him up again. For endless minutes he flails
and flounders, sinks, treads water, his body fights to breathe, he
scrambles and claws at the slick sides, failing; he is creature: abject,
terrified, fraught, until they haul him up choking and wrung. Reborn
then, theirs.

The children walked up the mountain and heard the terrible prophecies that must never be told. Why children were chosen for such a charge must test the heart. The boat is breaking up, pounded between sandbars in storm winds. You clutch at rails, the boat rolls, the masts are leaning, whip and moan. The wave lifts and falls, sickening, lets drop, then you are over the side, the water wild, how violently it swirls, tearing you under. A hand reaches down, you are grasped by your long, seaweed-floating hair and hauled to the surface. Clutched under arms and heaved into the lifeboat, gasping, clutching sky.

And we do not know the world, the cosmos reeled inside our minds. Miserable, mad, the prisoner's lips form syllables wrung through crushed breath. For these words, or what the inquisitor believes he hears, a witch is burned, an assassin condemned. We punish heresy with fire. Solar flares lick the dark, the northern lights soar, sign of works to come, and one rows the boat out on the still pond, one stands behind the lighted window, and one pours flame into water and water into flame, but denies the miracle.

6.

How I slept then, undone, sank with weight pressed into the bed, pressed flat and dry: papyrus, remnant of carbon breathing. That I might be written on. I slept for weeks of days, my flesh a shroud, a fine gauze laid across my bones. I slept, and kept the secret of bone, alive and intricate, streaked brown with marrow, blood and tissue of cells in honeycomb formation studded with salt and mineral crystals. My eyelids jerked and fluttered, electric volts of dream image passed unchecked across my brain's rutted landscape. Still I did not wake. Air of night, air of morning then, descended into me, remaking each cell, a loosening of bonds, each cell finding new space to breathe, a thousand discrete stirrings, the life within life. This is how the universe expands, each thing floating further from every other thing as the substance inflates with space. Silence a presence. Space not a nothing, presence of void. Time entered me then, I was not I. My mind's light dropped beneath the horizon, sank into my being like sunset, sank gratefully, resting on clouds that eased its fading. It was all light of cloud vapor and water, then dark. Then stars appeared.

I slept for years then, emptying. I did not leave my body—that was not yet. I did not go into a hare or a deer, or any other creature. I slept as earth rose into me, as sky leaned down, until I had no weight. No longer on, but in the earth. Became dry reed and leaf tissue, web of carbon, lattice of bone. That is one way of imagining. Atoms circled within themselves, the sensation of solid flesh, illusion of being, illusion we touch, reaching for the other, the beginning of separation.

7.

And now this morning, this fine first light, quick with gleam where it touches the kettle, the glass, spreading a blaze of gold across the floor. Light touches matter into life, its waves breaching space between heavenly bodies, at home in the dark density of being. Tea, and blueberries in a white bowl, the wood of the table silk with touch, the grain of the boards smoothed—what power restores me to myself, carries me back to my body now, redeemed? I woke where I fell. Set me square, right me as stone, fix me, settle weight of being here. Yes I have seen other worlds, innumerable lives and worlds and bodiless forms. Whirled, lifted, spun, let me rest in one self a while. And so I walked out and the air was only air I breathed and the bird on the branch did not regard me skew; the wrathful deities of the mind did relent, and further I was not pressed but was indulged in sun to rest, to open as a bud, a rose unfurled, rugosa white and pink, with dark and wrinkled leaves outspread—you would not know I had such soft, such opulent and sumptuous parts within me, nothing added only more revealed in opening, more upon more shown forth, the fragrance, the mystery of the flower in the bud. Though I am not a flower, I am a woman who may open into blossom only once and once forever, the body one world come now to settle in the moment that contains the world; it does not leave itself, only fulfills itself unfolding. I feel the falling into place, return, my thankfulness is great and contains a flower—even the earth I walk on must contain the flower, to scatter and spend the order furled within the bud, released not to return, we do not return, we go on, as they say it is not time passing, that time is and never was or will be, always is. It is order that passes, unfolding within this open time, this earth my feet today upon, I come to earth to live—oh body, you are earth to me.

VIII

Histories

I.

genome

Once we were one.
Then wandered, set feet forth
ahead and onward gone;
apart to walk, small bands to roam.
Northing to wind, and wending went
along rough ways. No path or road
then; there we were
wind without end, all scattered,
broken up, undone.

Once we were one. Like wind we bore,
were borne, were outward flung.
Sound waves from single drum.
In one time only, one, no time to come
until we break and go
out from this place away
into a land of dust and stars.
I show you kin,
clan, cousin, tribe: we wandered far,
we strayed to turn
life opening called beyond.

Now take him wife from neighbor's tent,
be onward gone.
Girl given stranger suffer mother's grief.
Break ties to bind, make new.
We must have lost to find,
to come upon, to know.
Be broken to know other, second, else,
in whom we find the other who is not
the self, toward whom the self
may bend. These strangers who
are not ourselves in whom
we find the lost again.

2.

invasions

Soars the boat now sails above
horizon, raises dragon's head,
beats wings of oars, roars up,
rides wave ashore, brings war
and fear to bear on nations seized:
(My terrible grandfather—Hello!)
And it was holy Toledo the Visigoth king
and holy the edicts and the tribunals.
We removed the old ones to make way for new:
all driven arriving, driving on.
Legions, pilgrims, nations destroyed.
(The savages died like rotten sheep . . . their bodies . . .
after death were exceedingly yellow.)
New dog park raises taxes, the town
fenced off the beach; red dory
on the sand a picture postcard, I was there
once defeated made picturesque.
Condoms high tide floated up deflate.
A memorial frieze lauds our birthright:
we came here fleeing ruin.

I forget my pills. The cat's pills I always remember.
Status this morning dire, lightning tremor in the nerves,
gunfire in the hills exploding.
A bowl of yellow apples, queue of green
tomatoes on the windowsill turning
their flanks to the sun. Such quiet in the garden
now when words are not returned,
each question eaten by sky.
We go into the woods with our captive Sacagawea,
a slave in fact, not reconciled.
This morning the dead speaking under the earth
not in words but listen:
underword of underworld, the absolute
is-ness and terror of their being.
Oh terrible forebears, the cost of exile
is exile. What is and is not, what is always
the death inside me that sings in my ear,
that shadows my dance, barefoot on the grizzly rug
by the fire in the great lodge winter nights.

3.

barbarian girl

I stood barefoot in a torn dress by a tarpaper shack in a starving coal
town. I was never any stranger's story. I stared straight into the camera. I
was once a barbarian among the stones of England. Eight hundred years
of tribal war. Before history was written here. When stones were raised
on the backs of slaves, and people burned for sacrifice. How our warrior
armies scared the Romans, who were no green troops, fighting their way
north for years. I remembered a river whose banks had never known a
city. Nettles and ferns, ramps and berries. Netting the small rabbits, a
barb to spear the glancing fish. On the island the sun falls off the edge
of the world. I carried seaweed up to a little garden. Later Vikings
landed on shore, killing many villagers and burning their huts; one of
these invaders became my great-great-grandfather. So I came to live.
Later the plague dead piled in heaps. A remnant survive. A remnant

and then a remnant of the remnant, and still we live. I stood in the doorway; see how my feet were bruised and twisted, how thin my arms crossed on my chest. Some brothers and sisters behind me, peering out: vacant faces of hunger. The shutter clicked once. In this picture everything I am is held; the world is whole behind my stare. The thousand years to come do not exist.

4.

because one did survive the wreck

When Wrath of God returned from his captivity among the barbarians, seven years after being kidnapped from his village by a trader, sold as a slave in Spain, ransomed by priests, and spirited to England where he was kept as a rich man's trophy,

then,

having talked his way onto a ship bound for Newfoundland, later to sail with Thomas Dermer's expedition down the coast where he was taken on as a translator, having learned English during his sojourn in London,

when,

having prevailed through patience and ingenuity, through many and diverse dealings with these nations and persons, each of whom had their own purposes concerning him, when after these hard years and great effort he reached his home, he found all lost.

The year after he was taken a great plague had swept the Atlantic seaboard, killing over 90 percent of the Wampanoag, Massachusetts, Pennacook, Nauset, Pemaquid, and Abenaki populations; from southern Maine to Narragansett Bay the coast lay empty. "Utterly void," wrote Dermer in his log.

His village, Patuxet, deserted, the houses empty, the fields overgrown. Bones of his family and neighbors lay whitening in open air, their skeletons bleached by the sun. The only words we have for this come down come from Europeans,

"In a place where many inhabited, there hath been but one left alive,
to tell what became of the rest, the living being (as it seemed) not able

to bury the dead, and they were left for crowes, kites, and vermin to
prey upon. And the bones and skulls upon the several places of their
habitations, made such a spectacle after my coming into those partes
. . . it seemed to me a new found Golgatha."   Thomas Morton

who often as not betray their own sympathies in the recounting,

"There hath, by God's visitation, reigned a
wonderful plague . . . in a manner to the utter
destruction, devastation, and depopulation of that
whole territory, so as there is not left . . . any that do
claim or challenge any kind of interest therein . . .
we, in our judgment, are persuaded and satisfied,
that the appointed time is come in which Almighty
God, in his great goodness and bounty towards us,
and our people, hath thought fit and determined,
that those large and goodly territories, deserted
as it were by their natural inhabitants, should be
possessed and enjoyed by such of our subjects."

King James I

and further:

"How strangely they have decreased by the Hand of God . . . and it hath
generally been observed that where the English come to settle, a Divine
Hand makes way for them."   Daniel Denton

"The savages died like rotten sheep, and their bodies before and after
death were exceedingly yellow."   Thomas Dermer

"He made a path for his anger; He spared not their soul from death, but
gave their life over to the pestilence."   Psalm 78:50

"In a short time after, the hand of God fell heavily upon the Nausets with
such a mortal stroke that they died on heaps as they lay in their houses."

Thomas Morton

"How doth the city sit solitary, that was full of people!"

Lamentations 1:1

"The woods were almost cleared of those pernicious creatures, to make room for a better growth."
Cotton Mather

"About four years ago all the inhabitants died of an extraordinary plague, and there is neither man, woman, nor child remaining: as indeed we find none to hinder our possession."
Mourt's Relation

"The wrath of God is a lamentation."
Abraham Heschel

When Wrath of God walked away from the ruins of his home, he had become a modern man. There had always been a way back in spite of obstacles—from Spain to London, and Newfoundland, his travels and captivity had been harrowing but focused toward an end. Now there was no place to return; his entire world was gone. He stood without context, without a useful past, in a kind of permanent exile, neither outside nor inside, in limbo, without definition.

It was a modern man who a year later strode into Plymouth, the English settlement built over the bones of his old home, and addressed the settlers—in good English, learned in the best of London society—to announce his name, Tisquantum, meaning "Wrath of God," a name perhaps chosen in this second incarnation. The Pilgrims would shorten this to "Squanto." As go-between between the Pilgrims and the surviving Wampanoag, he would negotiate treaties and translate trade agreements. The Pilgrims valued him as a guide and advisor. He existed for them in terms of their own world, a useful neighbor.

And he intrigued on both sides, demanding kickbacks from the Indians who wanted to trade with the newcomers, and conspiring to plant suspicion among all parties. Massasoit called him a man without a center. Massasoit, a premodern man, noble in the ancient way, grieved but not confused by events, did not trust him. Massasoit saw clearly, but like any mortal, he couldn't see the future.

As for the English, they were not modern, and did not wish to be modern, having fled the world of social change and revolution in their quest to restore an imagined purity of the first Church, to build their city on a hill, a theocracy in the wilderness while parsing their miniscule differences with the Church of England to an imagined gorge. Perched in the new world, they yet belonged to the old, in time as well as culture. Of the players here it is Tisquantum who most nearly models the world we know. The last survivor of Patuxet, a village erased from time, a soul untethered from his past, opportunistic, self-serving, solitary, and estranged, he prefigures our loneliness, our exiles and migrations, the displacement of peoples and endless search for foothold, before the history of this nation had even begun.

5.

famine ships

They came on ships, each of them, everyone who was not born here, for centuries they, that is, we, came here on ships. The ocean between worlds, empty for thousands of miles. So many across the gray wild ocean, this Atlantic. Slave ships, convict ships, famine ships, steamers, and sailing ships. Barks and brigs, liners and whalers . . .

and the great number below decks, listed: laborer, spinster, peasant, wife. Listed: Healthy Adult Male. Came with bundles, pots, and tools of trade. Convicts, indentured servants, masters and captains amassing fortunes in transport.

And the masters too had come on ships, and the captains, they too had had to come, to arrive, but first they needed to depart: thousands of farewells, exile, removal, flight. Evictions and clearances, a thousand Irish in one day at the port of New York, for years of days, fever in the folds of their clothes, and bodies stung with salt. How the sharks began to follow the boats when typhus flared among the crowded, starving passengers. Ship fever. Bones in the deep. A body wrapped in cloth, weighted with stones, the de profundis said over it, the plank tipped. Teeth and nails. Buttons and buckles. Very few diamonds I think were lost and much cargo saved but precious flesh swallowed by the ton. Husbands and wives, little children lost their lives. It was sad when that great ship went down.

                                  I love the beach but fear the ocean.
I walk at the edge of departure, testing the edge, but no further. How many separate voyages of ancestors bring me here? Why tease the odds further? Arriving is full of uncertainty, and welcome is a middling thing. What you have carried will not carry you, will not avail; you begin again, scourged and emptied. Arriving tests courage, but leaving scours the heart. Every arrival begins in refusal. In Ireland they would hold a wake for the one departing (I will never look on your face again, the mother said, weeping farewell), until there were too many dead and too many had sailed and the heart could bear no more.

                                Ocean, ocean . . . I call you by name
and I hear your voice of waves—ocean, ocean . . . liquid sound . . . the bleak mystery of moving over water, no way back. You are far out, that is to say—nowhere—you are forgotten—no one can reach you there. Where you have gone—where you are going—what is happening there—you are far out, far gone. When you go down what will raise you up—when you blow north—when you toss on your bunk in fever. Ocean, ocean . . . convey us,

                                bring us over. We come on ships, called to or expelled from. Fleeing, shackled, spat out. Papers in our coats we cannot read. Blood in our faces, memory in our blood, a little warmth there, in our blood, the ocean has none, sun dances on its surface, we sail, skimming, tossed, the further down the colder it grows, further and further, leaving land, leaving sky,

                                tumbling dark, losing those left behind.
Each of us stepped out—stepped onto a boat, stepped down the sharp curving stair, pressed from behind, clutching our bundles and our babes, and each of us stepped out into light, arrived here, though here was only a where to us then. The ones who never stepped out we do not continue; we are the children of survivors. Son leaves, arrives orphan. Wife arrives

widow. These are the ones who survive losing. We are the ones who came, which meant leaving, prerequisite to arriving. We came by ship over water and here it lies, ocean, ocean . . . still unknown, passage yet uncomprehended.

6.

clay

While the Angel of Death rides on the fumes of the iron scow, and infected airs are wafted to our shores from the anchorage, we shall have no security against these annual visitations of pestilence.

Dr. Anderson, 1858 *Harper's Weekly*

We the roughs, the unruly—promising little, failing much, we mumblers, dissemblers, despoilers of custom and courtesy, we

the issue of conquest, brood of indenture, the displaced of capital, delivered here from endless lineage of wretches begotten in desperate couplings in cellars and ships' holds, landed here to suffer and to clutch whatever is left by them to spare—

we the potato-fed, mush-tongued, spooning gruel over toothless gums, we, lumpen, swaybacked, basin-hipped, slit-grinned, with blemish, wen and pustule, who lick the grease from kingpin's palms, scavenge orts and offal, suckle pap

and live to bring forth children in pain and suffering, eat dust our days and break our backs with toil.

Son of man, eat what is given you.

We come bearing jaundice, influenza, typhoid and cholera, roseola, rickets, measles, pox and flux, like tribute for our betters, the surfeit of our being, our lice and fleas, our pinworms, hookworms and scrofula, our phlegms and humours. We are here on this shore bred in multitudes, we are always with you now.

It is spoken that salvation is free. We hold precisely nothing in our hands. We testify in open air, a vagrant crown, a tentless mind.

It is spoken that the landless will be driven to the river to be baptized because there is on earth no place for us to stand.

You—we—mine—and it is spoken that the slave led forward into exile finds self when slave in self has died.

And none of that generation who crossed the parted waters, who walked on the dry land between the waves, were left alive to see that promised land.

Still, we are a stiff-necked people ungrateful and defiant, trusting none, our own worst friend. Give me a rope, I'll make a noose. Show me a height, I'll dash myself. All knives kept under lock. The voice of the orphan in mind insisting: suffer. Eat bread and drippings.

The robber baron locks up his manse. Throws out crust and bones. Their horses bred to run, and Pinkertons, nice name for a brute, set against the workers who stood at Homestead.

Yet we will murder the one who dares to say we are the protoplasm of creation, that we fill the sky with light.

We bred with Neanderthals, a noble race who live in us yet. They too were stardust. And the taste of ash at Dachau soldiers carried on their clothes, an ocean of ash, and the woman standing at a long window above the gardens in a room fitted out for the visit of Marie, queen of Romania, granddaughter of Victoria, long to reign over us, a room in the mansion of the great railroad mogul, who bought the window and the view, who bought the queen's visit,

a tired woman with a dust rag in her hand pauses to gaze at view of hillsides dense with trees that have always been there and once belonged to no one.

lineages

"Descended from royalty," my mother would say, reinventing family history over gin and seconal. I wouldn't brag if it were me. Some poor scullery maid straight from the workhouse, got with child by a randy young nephew of some duke or lord. Surprised her behind the cinders where he pulled up her skirt to see what was what. When her belly swells she's sent packing from the great house. How low can you fall from second scullery maid? Her child born in squalor, the precious jewel the gene useless without the name. It all comes down from the father.

Dirty she was, grimed with soot and grease and weeks-old sweat—but so was he, all the English happily unwashed—a great democracy of lice—the smell of them would disgust the clean and handsome Indians, who could barely stand to have them in their houses. Not to mention their faces full of hair.

Perhaps he, the forebear, the lordling, younger son of a younger son, grew up to sail for the colonies, to some island or plantation granted by the king, where to re-create feudal splendor and comfort, serfs are needed. For serf read slave. And there to prosper, freely bestowing his seed on native women, African slaves and white servants alike, all who kept his fields and horses, his house and barns, and laid his table and scrubbed his floors, and made him rich. If there is "noble" lineage on this shore, it is because the owners are fathers of all they covet. The top ape procreates. How we are mingled in blood of hierarchy, given over to dominion.

And dominion is domain, the land owned before it was claimed. She arrived indentured seven years, her child to be raised in service. Did she sign or was she taken? "Spirits" prowled the London slums, to lure and sometimes kidnap the hapless or desperate poor, offering food and drink and promises of easy work. Sign the contract and you'd find yourself locked up until the ship could sail, already owned, unfree.

Meanwhile he, our first progenitor, father of thousands unchronicled, disappears from the history. How can we claim the father? He must own us or we are not. The father gives himself whether he stays or goes but the birthright is reserved.

* * *

If our fathers were conquerors, our mothers were slaves. Rape splinters the past. And yet, and yet . . . nations are born. La Malinche—traitor and mistress of Cortés, mother of a new people, womb and breast, a tortured lullaby. Marina, Llorona, Chingada . . . for us, given: her ruin. Five hundred years. The conqueror owns the future, our bodies spoils of war.

In war, rape is a crime against the fathers. How can we claim the usurper in us? A nation with two hearts.

This cannot be unwound.

* * *

A foundling cannot become a prince, but may be king through conquest—may rise, and forget his original state, forbid it to be spoken of, and live to bestow title on his son, while the blood of lost ancestors cries to him, "My child!"

A man might believe he is his days, and call the nights another world, and long for a life of trumpets, forgetting his flesh, forgetting the beast that is holy in him, the creature with a spirit to redeem him.

Finding ends searching. Follow the creases in the map instead of the roads; you don't know where you're going anyway.

The son of a conqueror may be a prince, may live to be king. Or he may be a foundling, sent on a ship to serve empire, abandoned on the hills with his heels pierced, or cast into desert exile. Ishmael, the firstborn, owned Abraham's blessing. His favorite, Sarah's bane. But Isaac was tricked and Jacob stole his brother's birthright. The women of patriarchy all vying for their children's claims, the father's blessing, wiles and deception . . . what does the mother have to give but life?

A daughter may be sold for sheep, may go with the stranger and never see her home. Eighteen indentured servants sailed on the *Mayflower*, four of them children. Good Quaker whalers refitted their ships for the slave trade and funded that brutal passage. The president's son in the slave quarters, learning to make nails . . .

IX

The Book of Mystery

I.

Again birds are flying. They float into view and are gone.
White and dark, they inscribe the sky, their wings
imply an absence. How every going
leaves an emptiness where you stood, days lost inside other days,
the tease of horizon retreating.

For weeks now nothing: window of sky.
If only the wind would come up, toss world to lie in jumble,
break, remake . . . let clouds and grasses flirt,
feint in sunrays' shifts, play hide and flee with light . . .
but the day is calm.

The birds fly over; they fly past.
They make me feel the edge of sight
where world goes on unanchored.
Two figures are moving on the hill.
They appear along the ridge, rising as they approach.
They pause, then turn and go off another way,
descending a slope into green understory.
Space expands in all directions, no center,
and I am not inside or outside of anything.
Reaching to touch something that doesn't disappear.

Everything disappears.
A rail on a ship churning forward in high seas.
Hold on and ride the swells; you are not held
but driven forward, sky bending into ocean, gray
into gray and mist into wave. The wind pushes,
it blows you back. Gulls beat the air like omen.

At sea, birds mean land. Can you make out a shape
in the distance, a home there? A wave or a wall?
Birds found the island first. It was an island of birds.
Were there insects then to feed them,
worms bred out of rot, spontaneous generation of flies
from sea foam, as Aristotle said?
How do things come to be where there is nothing?

What book, what history to hold? A wall of rock.
People digging out a tunnel
to meet another tunnel underground; if they veer,
if they turn the slightest bit aside,
they will dig deeper forever, each beyond
the place of the other's beginning.

I will be lost in God, not found,
the dread of him who is no home.

2.

   A strange insect shaped like a hermit crab, two arms outstretched
like pincers, a tiny tank of a bug, crawled out from the binding of my
book when I opened it. The book had been closed upright on a shelf
between books. How long was this creature lost between pages 52
and 53, and why wasn't it crushed there? How does it live? Does it eat
paper—or glue? Could it stroll in and out at will? I blew on it, hoping
to lift it from the page with my breath, and it collapsed in a sticky ball,
then slowly stretched open again, one hair-thin leg and then another,
and went on walking. It walked across a line of Santōka's haiku. The
verse read: "Going deep / and still deeper / into green mountains." The

space between things is infinite, atoms or galaxies. These pages pressed together may circumscribe a boundary but nothing can measure the space within space itself. Within which the creature moves. Always a gap, in which possibility may flare. The insect was the size of the letter *m* on the page. I closed the book gently and a moment later it reappeared, balanced along the outermost edge of the pages, still walking.

3.

in the morning the fish swim to the surface of the water to drink the light. they rise magically inside the water, a blossoming, a sparkle. to be part of such brightness, the dazzling fish in every dimension rising and falling, how on earth we scuttle along a plane, burdened, turning here and there and back and forward bearing the weight of air. another world this element so close I could have reached out my hand but did not know. the fish swim just below the surface in the light, and join and quickly part, and eggs like iridescent bubbles fall so lightly down, shimmering in their multitudes, so many not all will be eaten this is paradise world light and dark the body made buoyant, and the bright fish swim away their bodies waving

4.

So I went out on the hill with a mug of hot coffee.
It was early morning, the blackbirds hadn't yet
started up their chatter. Steam rose so simply
from the whole surface of the dark brew, and warmed
my face when I lifted it to drink.
Then a wire in my mind was tripped,
a buzz and a fumbling, and a voice spoke.

What do you want? the spirit said. It was one of
those questions designed to test you. So I looked at
the steam rising, water going to air without effort
or will, and I said: *Let me rise.*

I could feel that this wasn't a good answer.
And what kind of game was this, so early in the morning,
some catechism my twice-broken brain invented
out of electric currents, or was the voice real?
I thought for a minute
and decided to respect the question.
Again: *What do you want?*

To come to the end of myself.

5.

dwell

Every moment in you, every cell of being sheltered
there.
No place in you that does not know me, that will not have me whole.

Noon: the whistle sounds from town,
a small plane rises into clouds
the sound of engines going off in the distance.

I feed myself slices of apple with one hand,
palm open my book with the other.
The sound of engines softens, growls and purrs.
Within that new quiet, the suck of waves.
Inside me the leaving, sky vanishing into sky,
no place where it is not.

The sky is pearl, and not a vacancy.
Black seeds on a white plate,
white apple, mottled skin . . . the knife cutting fruit.
And a thought of the missing one, absent so long,
closes time—though time is not a circle.

To become who you are not
you have to leave who you are.
Reading the book of the beloved,
who must withdraw, to be called again.
The mystery, the nowhere of between
when every moment light begins from darkness.
When I empty my lungs there is space inside me,
then I breathe and am full of being. Dwell
in the place between. That moment
alive and empty. To fall, and falling find
no place that is not here.

6.

All inside now, a fish inside a sea, water dense bearing me inside
salt current's flow. Close valves. Black, black, susurrant . . . there are
highways forever lit, iridescence of taillights, ghost trails vapor spun. A
sea is not the sky. Sea where I founder, washed back and forth in waves,
cradle that is a heart. The sky has no mother. Curled in the greater body,
held inside what I cannot feel the shape of—borne beneath storm surge;
muscle of water, its weight and urge pushes me, presses, forms swirl of
galaxies, swirl of prophecy, pressed in my brain. Speak, and the world
is devoured. Night into day we are told to keep watch. There was a door
in the earth, a stone stair winding under. A dream of leaves falling. The
shadow of the mountain drowns in night, the plane lights blink in air.
Here there is no breath.

7.

When I had died and stood nowhere,
outside of moments, gathered
beside myself, undoing,
vanishing into undone,
I was surprised. I always believed

there would be one more thing. One moment
had always followed on another,
always something coming after.

I searched in what remained of memory for images.
Already the swirl was scattering what I knew.
Like ash, like leaves, like birds released.
Already people and places mingling
equally, remembered and imagined.
My first lover, a patch of weeds behind a shed,
the low sun firing the branches of trees beside the pond.
There were other visions, too, partial and brief,
which seemed to belong to other lives not mine,
the whirlwind erasing distinctions.

Only one thing stood clear. I saw my great white dog
who walked with me nine years on wooded paths,
years when I was so lonely
only his silence could comfort me.
I saw him up ahead on the trail packed hard with snow.
He was nosing at a stump, getting news.
Even then he never walked beside me, but circled
out and back, allowing me the gravity
of a moving center. When he died he left an emptiness
carved into air. The silence of his being
could not be gathered up. He simply was no more.

Now I was gone.
Going. Gone. Still going. I was, I said, surprised.
Had I come all this way for this,
to see nothing added or subtracted
from being, to be shown that nothing mattered,
no account remaining in the infinite equation?
Could this be all, to simply stop?
Yes. The word hung, and disappeared
in the emptiness: nothing less
could be large enough.

The Prophecy of the Dead

1.

silent hooded figures
shades flit and moan

the crossroad the blood tree
the face in the stone

how did you go there
what did you see

the face in the stone
the blood tree

2.

    I sat beside the road with everything I carried, waiting for my ride. Morning traffic swept the highway; some cars still had their headlights on. I drew with a stick in the dirt at my feet. I was happy. The first people did this, scratched with a stick in the dirt. No waiting then, no highway, no clock or sweep of lights. When time was full of moments.
    Sunlight flashed through the leaves, but soon it would rain. The air felt heavy. Clouds blew across the sky, thin, broken by blue; light shuttered through them. Time hurried as the light flicked off and on; clouds blew across the sun and the air went dark, then bright again.

All this will be here when I die, I thought. The light through the trees glittered eagerly in this knowledge. It was as if I had finally said out loud what everyone was thinking. Then I could see past myself a moment, just a glimpse out of the moment and past time. One day I was not here, and another day I will not be here again. My heart beats, my lungs take in air, I eat the body of the world and I am gone.

I scratched with a stick in the dirt, sitting there with my possessions at my back: clothes and food, a few books, and things for writing. All I would need. How many others have sat here or walked on this ancient patch of earth, and now they are gone and I know nothing of them? Moments they had, waiting or walking, standing by a road, sitting on the ground, or passing through. Yet their lives were full to them. They wanted happiness. They felt their lives were real and so they were, yet like anyone's, empty and perishing.

I could feel myself dissolving. To be a tree or a stick, or a yellow van passing on the road. Looking up into the trees with their small leaves, each holding a spot of sun. Not the leaf but the meeting place of sun and green . . . for the first time understanding I have not always been here, will not always be. And other people will be here, and walk and stand or wait, and they will know nothing of me.

It is always the obvious confounds me. Things everyone seems to know and take for granted hit my mind like revelation. I am speaking here of loss, though just a moment ago I called it happiness. How joy springs up within sadness, like grass piercing the earth. Because I was sitting by the road and all the life I knew was ended. There was an empty space in my thoughts that allowed this understanding.

Looking up into the trees, sun making the leaves golden. There was no leaf, no sun, no green, but all of these appeared and passed and returned again, only changed. I sat by the side of the road with my back against a tree and watched the early traffic pass. My possessions lay piled at my side. I drew with a stick in the dirt. No images or words, but signs—circles, lines, dashes. It was not a map but a secret language, unknown even to me because it had not yet taken form. It was the beginning. Ants in the sand, midges in the air, midsummer. How many eons to gain one human life? I drew a circle in the dirt and erased it with my foot, then drew a spiral, and an X, then three solid and broken lines like runes. Lines began to join other lines. Circles opened and were broken. This went on and on, telling the story of time, the way the rough

bark of the trees folded into itself and the huckleberry leaves danced
on thin stems and sky fell through the branches of the pines. In that
moment I felt a happiness that was not like any happiness I knew before.
I could not hold it as it hovered over me, it was too new, too strong, too
free. World without end, I said, and died into it, amazed.

3.

bardo

Be not fond of the dull smoke-colored light from hell.

Under dune heights: swale, heath,
   spurges, stunted
oak and pine I am taller than.
   Gray lichen, puffball, reindeer moss,
roots that have failed
   upholding. Black pine-
cones, seeds spent, no road here,
   buzzard circling
bare knob of hill, coyotes
   yip in the distance.
Your prints,
   shallow, remain
—nothing will grow
   where you walk, every step gouges
the sand, tears at this slenderest
   membrane fiber
life.

A spider scuttles up a rock and falls back.
   I adjust my pack, drink lukewarm
water from a flask, taste of tin.
   I sit down and open the small
blue notebook: It is written,
   you will walk here until you see

the desert bloom, until your eyes see all
        changed. Reveal
the plenty in the gaps, these plants
        older than ice age, surviving,
this rock ensouled.
        The vesper sparrow, the spider's veil.
And here
I can do nothing. Pass through the air.
        Become nowhere.

4.

Bird sounds. It is the old ones calling me back; they have to borrow
voices because theirs have died. Today they are crows. How they clamor
and squawk; they mutter and gabble and moan complaint. So many
lives to remember. When Mongolia battled to the rim of Europe. After
hunters walked up out of Africa. A hard life in the north country then,
the ice crawling back toward the poles; nothing grew on certain slopes
but lichen and moss. I had a basket woven of reeds, I foraged among
the bracken, I turned over rocks for grubs, picked leaves, and dug the
roots of herbs. I did not have a comb for my hair, or a woven blanket, or
grain kneaded into bread. Yet I felt that that life was whole, it was ample
and not lived in any dearth, the light of mind alive in my being, sweet
sunlight and the touch of flesh on mine.

The old ones are afraid they will disappear forever into shadow where
they cannot feel themselves. Ghost substance sublimed in air. They
want me for their eyes, their fingers, their breath. They sent me here,
the mothers and fathers, into this future, this life they would claim. You
are too many I tell them, too many to carry, you must be content to lie in
the ground. In time where nothing is lost. But everything gets jumbled
up together there, they complain. They don't want to end. They croon
that they will care for me, warm me, and feed me but their need sucks
and pulls. They say they own me, but I am not fooled. I know that they
are crows.

ghost

He is no more here than a footprint lifted from a dry riverbed a thousand years old.

A motion that changes the shape of space, a weight and an intention passing. The dead are here but not in space.

And light is a something, a traveler between worlds, shape-shifter, bodiless body, wave and dust swept, heaped like grains of sand like moonshine honey: spirit is particle and pulse but never both together.

The spirit in form is burdened, slow-circling, encountering itself over and over, the dance weaving space.

I saw him clear as he were standing here before me muscle and breath, smell of oilcloth, the weight on the air that is a man.

Moonlight splashed on the floor rippled through clouds overhead, soft.

Light is a traveler only known when it arrives.

It was like hearing music when there is no space between the notes because they hum beyond their striking, and because the space between the notes is music too.

He struck a tinder from a metal box and lit his pipe. He sat forward and leaned his arms on the table.

Sometimes a wall is a door.

And a portal may open on only one side to disclose a world that does not see you and goes its way its rounds unregarding.

6.

The Captain lies in the other room,
his body large and square. Blue coat,
brass buttons, the watch fob
threaded in his fat stiff fingers.
His eyes downcast
as if he were about to check the time
but someone closed them, he's looking inward.
In fact they might have taken his eyes,
why not, they're no good to him now.
I have custody of the corpse
who dominates the house, demanding notice.
An oppression from the other room
as a great will still willing,
a tide past flood that won't stop rising.

7.

at the white station

    I am seated among the surfmen at the long table. The room
is cold, and pale with chalky light. The bread tastes of dust. A gray
speckled pot squats on the table, brimming a pale chowder thick with
potatoes and onions. A fish-head floats in the broth, enormous, as large
as a dog's head, bobbing askew with one eye staring up. A voice says:
potatoes are the meat of the dead.
    The fish, and the translucent chunks of onion floating,
everything white, and the gray spar of spine protruding from the severed
neck. The head floats like a sunken boat, nose upward. Gray scales, white
flesh in broth, white gum of bones.
    We pass bowls without speaking, clink of chinaware and
spoons. The spoons are huge, barely small enough to fit in our mouths,
with very short handles, we have to grip them in our fists.
    Coffee is poured, white and milky, into white mugs. Sugar
falling like stars from tiny spoons. I am cold, cannot taste the soup that
passes over my tongue dissolved like fog, like cold mist.

A man is playing cards at the end of the table, some solitaire game, turning the cards over one by one, absorbed, as if each motion was utterly interesting but not urgent. He deciphers fate who is outside of fate, removed beyond occasion. Finally someone takes down a guitar shaped like a teardrop, and plays. He begins singing in a language I don't understand. The music is sad and strong. A guitar, a cracked human voice that sings past me into the hearts of the dead fathers, and though I am favored to attend, I do not learn their secrets.

XI

Water of Night

I.

Water of night,
>   gaze transparent
>   —as water is transparent,
not clear, but many-layered,
>   with ripples swelled from locus outward,
complicating figure and ground.

Vibrant the bounce dance of molecules, matter
>   stirred within, stirring up
>   ghost particles of former lives—we were once
>   water,
>   reflecting star-
>   light in sharp points,
>   dancing
>   across broken surface, this one
>   day star, ours, its gaze
>   broken, become myriad.

>   Reflections on the surface
return the gaze to the gaze; my eyes see my eyes'
reflection, and through them the image of fish
>   swimming, and other fish
>   still deeper, glancing among the shoals;

and below,
>   the rocky bottom, shifting in light and shadow.

>   And water's currents also visible
as lighter and heavier densities
>   —wave line of greens and grays—
an awkward glob of seaweed lumbering loose-
>   limbed as a many-armed animal—
soft living thing
>   borne on salt water.

2.

When seeing into is seeing through.
Night, no lights in the shack.
Awake I swim out
>   beyond the black windows, buoyed
in black air, etheric body, wave and wonder,
and all is changed.

Vision shifts like film laid over film,
ghost signs fading,
>   gestures of other worlds.

This room for instance: a vessel,
ship fitted out for Valhalla, or China,
or following a ghost run of cod
into the cold waters of Georges Bank.

I am no sailor
but they've given me the wheel;
the hold is full, no harbor here,
night falling, the waves
strike high, the boat rides heavy in the water
—steady! oh stay!—
I have no map but I steer ahead, straight on
into the black wall of night.

*   *   *

From Greenland ventured
into the Ocean Called Dark,
the ship wanders underworld of fog so thick
and constant: "numbing ocean's dark mist."
Ice, and winds blown down from north:
O Wind the Wailer the Whistler the coldly dressed.
Waverer, Wolf of the Sail:
they sailed—one thousand years—
a land of vines and fruit, to this rich land.

A woman stood here holding a child,
first born of new world. The old world
watched from wilderness.

*   *   *

No moon. The night watch stumbles,
shines his torch along a log
tossed in surf among black waves.
Starlight flirts through clouds
catching white tips of breakers.
The wind seethes, scratching up sand.
Out in the surf, the boat is caught between bars;
it lurches, pounded, pitched, and swung
in waves that leap and paw the air.
Crewmen clutch, haul lines,
the ship breaking up beneath them.
They try to launch the shore boat
—quick!—
                a great wave breaks
across the decks, and after,
                       an empty sea.

3.

On the table a cup and a book.
On the chair a towel folded twice.
Red bathing suit limp on the hook.
I swam today, I dove in air, floated in water.
I walked on the bottom of the sea,
met wonders.

Now I get up and light a match in the dark,
set the kettle over a ring of blue flame.
This night, this waking,
hangs inside the bubble of all possibles,
a float marking the water
that will not hold a mark. All worlds
are real, and are overcome,
are passed or passing; I cannot hold.

A plane swims in and out of clouds, blinking.
Down in the swale the coyotes barking,
there beyond that dire river,
past a hundred spirits of the dead
that no one wants to raise. Their faces are burned,
their fingers ash, their houses are no more.

I touch the red swimsuit,
still damp from the ocean. Yes,
I am alive. I walk to the door,
and stand leaning against the screen.
Dunes billow black below, black sea
with waves of shade and shadow.
Water of night, you could fall
off the edge of the world. One step and gone:
monsters, sea serpents, and no sailor returns.

4.

And who are these sleepers I see,
        the fierce ones gone quiet, the dead
                at rest like children
tucked up in beds, enraptured
by journey? And the still living:
my beloved grown old—these many years—
I put my hand out to touch
his sleeping breast rising
                and falling; he is tender
as he sleeps, sailing
in immensity.

My enemy is innocent
inside the water of night, no longer herself,
striving, edging for advantage, but content,
journeyed into being, her hand under her cheek
self-cradled, her face blank, without intending.

I swam today. I walked
beside the ocean and into the ocean,
water covered me. I walked
on the bottom of the world
that shifted with currents and was never still,
the ledge dropping off underfoot,
abrupt descent into deep
where I sank and was lifted. I lay rocked
in wave, borne up on swell pulse,
the pull and drag of moon's sky weight
calling the waters upward, so willing
to be called, to rise and fall
enchanted by a distant body sensed in cells,
world calling to world. And here

on the first dune, lofted above the beach
the grasses are sleeping under clouds,
the moon not yet risen to enthrall the sea meadow:

grasses in witches' dance shining white and black,
hurrying away from themselves, their tips seize and shudder
in air.
      Now air moves them
lightly, only to sway and bend, whispering
remembered syllables, the vast congregation of grasses
repeating one long motion, a sigh
that travels the hill's crest.

Black knot of the bayberry, cluster
of leaf and branch,
and the red-winged blackbirds' nest
lodged deep inside, baffled, hidden
in leaves, the birds asleep, five eggs, warm,
life waiting in them. Splash of waves on sand
unbroken beat sounds
inside the cells of things, varied soft and loud.
A trawler out past the bars
rides at anchor, single light hung up on her mast,
signal lifted and falling, no stars.

5.

Go out into the night, go out
like a candle; I lose
myself here, free wanderer, bare
soul regards
the sleepers, you who sleep,
not born to yourself.

Will you wake
with me—not to your dayself
      but here, in this rendezvous
where we leave off our history,
      where we have no face.

                    Will you wake,
original EveAdam—
                    first world—will you come?
I would not hold you or prevent
your going ahead
        or stopping to linger behind.
I would like
your company I invite.
Souls to rise, floated easy on water of night,
equal dark and shadow
on every form, strong weight
of landscape unmoving, electric nub
of objects holding themselves separate
yet also floating, we are carried
as we go, all things assist and forward us here.

                        6.

If you come I will show you
the bird with dragonfly wings
drawn in profile, one black eye
staring fixed on some prey,
black glossy feathers on his almond-shaped head,
long tatter of tail, trailing.

If you come I will show you
a woman in a long skirt, twirling.
The silk of her skirt makes a fountain,
                    at her feet, pouring,
            streams overlapping,
            so many shapes in a moment
and she goes on, twirling
in an empty room with no lights,
this scrap of dream image
rescued whole into world.

I will show you the sleeping city
that sleeps in its past
        in every moment that has been
up to this moment, and imagined beyond.
When houses were built by men's hands
and what is remembered—and not remembered—
all times at once, folds into its sleep, all stories
reconciled, where all must be
or nothing is.

All the dead and the forgotten
sleeping inside the city also.
And the small white fox
watching below your window,
hungry spirit, your familiar, the form
that moves past the corner of your eye
like shadow, that calls you down
the narrow staircase, past where the old ones sleep.
Will you wake and come with me,
and read the single dream the city is dreaming
and walk inside it, wandering
the old streets together? I will show you

the lilac that grew by the fence
        and the little bat hanging in the furthest
corner of the garden shed, self-swaddled,
the heavy lock
hung askew, half-secured by two nails
in the soft wood of the cellar door. I will show you
the place where nothing is lost because nothing
is; where we are emptied, witness
in wonder, knowing
all world in one. I would like
your company there, silent, amazed.
Your showing forth, your epiphany,
your calm.

            *   *   *

7.

Can you sleep? Are you sleeping?
Shh.
You aren't sleeping.
It's too hot.
You turned off the AC.
I wanted to smell the ocean.
The ocean? You mean the harbor.

All I can smell is onions from the hot dog stand.

I can't believe how many people are on the street this late. They're all drunk.
Roistering. That's a good word. Roistering.

My shoulders ache. I think I got too much sun today.

Are you sleeping?
Yes.
Do you want some chips?
OK.
I had a really good time today. I did.

Let's rent bikes tomorrow.
There is no tomorrow. We're on vacation.
Have a chip. I turned on the air so we can get some sleep.
Don't wake me at all in the morning. I want to sleep as long as I can. I want to waste the whole day. Then we'll go swimming and not take showers and I can smell the damn ocean without opening the windows.

If you go out for breakfast bring me something back.

XII

Boletes in September

Pine needles fallen across the path
cushion footfalls; rich brown loam mixes with sand, fine and silver-
gray beneath. Down and down, the world with its whole sorry history
scuffed and trodden underfoot: lithosphere, biosphere, the air suffused
with cloud, with water and dust, huckleberry leaves reddening, and
wintergreen pushing up small shiny leaves at the base of the pitch pines.
A taste of pine and salt on the air—how odors become us, absorbed as
molecules through the spongy, blood-rich tissue of nose and tongue, of
throat and sinus, into the deep, intricate cavities of our lungs with their
wet plush membranes, warm with our breath played across swelling
capillaries, the blood's own freshening; that's how the dead come into
us, through us, the same rich air recycled through ages—and what eats
the dead releases the past: nitrogen, carbon, minerals . . . so we are all
necrophages, devouring the sacrifice.

Here now, summer's last moment,
complete. The seed spills, burst from the flower, and acorns drop;
nothing has begun to die yet. Mast, duff, leaf litter, pinecones opening,
and dust of their pollens floated on air. And the mushrooms insane,
insensible, springing up with their fleshy genital swellings and
fluorescing hues, their astonishing blues and golds, spotted, speckled,
finned, egg-shaped, toylike, some still tearing the veil hung in tatters
about their stems like skirts, like skin, divine flesh risen from the dirt,
fed on the death of leaves, swelled, puffed, fattened on air. Kingdom
of fungi, five million species, more animal than plant, cryptic—of the

crypt. From the mycelium netted underground the filament of hyphae threaded neat. The primordia a bud, swelling, that pushing up ruptures the veil to surface in light.

Here boletes, the spongy ones, pale underneath—not the ones that stain blue or red when you touch them: *Boletus luridus*, *Boletus satanas* . . . but the pale brown ones—given us to eat. These arise from earth, burgeon, and deliquesce in days, brief as manna in the wilderness, this corruptible flesh. A fleeting boon, a benison—in a day it will perish, and stink with rot.

Some mushrooms you dare not touch, the poison on a fingertip sufficient harm. You may take food or poison up from the earth, and the poison too has value—as magic or medicine, it offers gateways to other worlds, not always fated. Choose your way wisely, aware. Some fruits are given you to eat, but of these you must not eat or you will surely die. My friend taught me these secrets, and more as well, in his exuberant old age, when we walked the woods and marshes and he instructed me in more ways than one. How things go out of themselves, and are not lost, that we walk among layers of time, and that to leave a place or a season is also to arrive.

Meanwhile things appear where they will, with no order to their appearing—or rather a great order, but hidden under leaves and roots. And a great order also in the sky, the planet turning in and out of the sun's penumbra, days and seasons. But I look at the ground and I say *scattered*, I say *strewn*, and *flung*, and such words as these, because I cannot see the deeper connections that lie beyond my ken. I'm like a dot on a plane, when in another dimension I would be a line across a field, and then a cone uniting coordinates in curved space, and so on. I know what I'm told—sometimes that's all. These mushrooms are death eaters, and don't we all eat the dead—yet these seem psychotic to me, with their misshapen, lumpy, mottled, withering, bloated shapes, decked out with full unseemly glee. But of course they are good, they are godly, I could preach them a sermon and they would carry the word faithfully back into the underworld where they return, as they do, dissolving back into earth undone, and the good news carried along the fibers to comfort the dead: "We come to undo you and release all you held; the rock lifted from your back you soar upward easily, you row the air and ascend."

In the desert Yahweh told the Israelites that the manna, godly food, heaven's fruit, was given only for the day. Sweet to the taste, and you must gather only what you will eat by nightfall and throw the rest away; by morning it will stink and crawl with maggots. Instruction for a wandering people, anathema to these poor so freshly out of bondage.

The manna, dissolved back into underworld, nourishes the dark river there, and what comes to the wanderer is only a handful of bread, a mouthful of air, honey on the tongue, but nothing you may keep. He wanted them to rely on Him only, you see. Every sundown nothing left but God—holyholyholy—why did they journey forty years in the desert—the way was not so long, but he confounded them, led them to wander in circles, to quarrel among themselves, and make gestures toward government, to wander outgrowing memory, until that whole generation that had been slaves died in the wilderness. From slave to self, the self forged . . . no home but God. Some things you cannot carry with you but they took Joseph's bones up out of the Nile and brought them forward, to fulfill the promise that he would not lie in tyrant's soil.

These Hebrews, which name means a kind of nomad, did not yet have a book; there was no temple, not even a code of law, just some commands sent down from an invisible god who spoke through smoke and fire and could not be found anywhere on earth. Memories of fathers leaving, called by a voice that would not name itself. Lech-Lecha, go, rise and leave this place, to Abram, to Jacob, now to a whole people. I will make you a nation. The manna, the water from the rock, and a people come out of bondage . . . my friend, that old man who taught me much, left the shtetl still a boy to make his way across Europe and sail here, living along this shore a long life still wandering, searching, gathering, who showed me where to find blueberries and beach plums, boletes, and cranberries, and to tell me in cold November when it was good to pick the mussels, purple and clacking softly along the rocks of the breakwater. Home is knowing how the land can feed you, he said. He had known hunger. And now I wander, out the fire road giving way to sand where the dunes open and trees part to sky. Behind me the pitch pines' tortuous branches wind and bend, struggling to stand in salt winds. The wind is a ghost, soughing in the trees—a voice calls—I look back but there's nothing. I carry his bones, that were burned to ash and became air, I carry them in my breath and blood, bone of my bone, and others too, the ancestors, the forgotten, the great and the small, become me. He taught me the invisible is most true, and can be known by the things of earth but only fleetingly, a glimpse of God's hindquarters as he vanishes into the cleft of the rock. I eat the bread of morning and food of earth, and at night I lie down and give back what I held—all my days.

ACKNOWLEDGMENTS

My thanks to the following journals in which poems or earlier versions of poems from *Terra Nova* have appeared: *Ecotone, Five Points, Hypothetical,* and *Orion.*

I am grateful to the Vermont Arts Council for a grant that aided in the completion of this work. Deep thanks are owed to the Fine Arts Work Center in Provincetown for several Returning Residency opportunities, which were crucial in forming this book and its memories. For reading and commenting on this work as it took shape, I am forever indebted to Jim Carpenter, Mark Cox, John Donaghy, Phil Pochoda, and David Wojahn. Thanks also to Ed Van Dorn for the gypsy.